**New Directions for
Teaching and Learning**

Marilla D. Svinicki
EDITOR-IN-CHIEF

R. Eugene Rice
CONSULTING EDITOR

# Scholarship of Multicultural Teaching and Learning

Matthew Kaplan
A.T. Miller
EDITORS

Number 111 • Fall 2007
Jossey-Bass
San Francisco

SCHOLARSHIP OF MULTICULTURAL TEACHING AND LEARNING
*Matthew Kaplan, A.T. Miller* (eds.)
New Directions for Teaching and Learning, no. 111
*Marilla D. Svinicki*, Editor-in-Chief
*R. Eugene Rice*, Consulting Editor

Microfilm copies of issues and articles are available in 16mm and 35mm, as well as microfiche in 105mm, through University Microfilms, Inc., 300 North Zeeb Road, Ann Arbor, Michigan 48106-1346.

NEW DIRECTIONS FOR TEACHING AND LEARNING (ISSN 0271-0633, electronic ISSN 1536-0768) is part of The Jossey-Bass Higher and Adult Education Series and is published quarterly by Wiley Subscription Services, Inc., A Wiley Company, at Jossey-Bass, 989 Market Street, San Francisco, California 94103-1741. Periodicals postage paid at San Francisco, California, and at additional mailing offices. POSTMASTER: Send address changes to New Directions for Teaching and Learning, Jossey-Bass, 989 Market Street, San Francisco, California 94103-1741.

*New Directions for Teaching and Learning* is indexed in CIJE: Current Index to Journals in Education (ERIC), Contents Pages in Education (T&F), Current Abstracts (EBSCO), Educational Research Abstracts Online (T&F), ERIC Database (Education Resources Information Center), Higher Education Abstracts (Claremont Graduate University), and SCOPUS (Elsevier).

SUBSCRIPTIONS cost $85 for individuals and $209 for institutions, agencies, and libraries in the United States. Prices subject to change. See order form at end of book.

EDITORIAL CORRESPONDENCE should be sent to the editor-in-chief, Marilla D. Svinicki, Department of Educational Psychology, University of Texas at Austin, One University Station, D5800, Austin, TX 78712.

Wiley Bicentennial Logo: Richard J. Pacifico

www.josseybass.com

# CONTENTS

# From the Series Editor

*About This Publication.* Since 1980, *New Directions for Teaching and Learning (NDTL)* has brought a unique blend of theory, research, and practice to leaders in postsecondary education. *NDTL* sourcebooks strive not only for solid substance but also for timeliness, compactness, and accessibility.

The series has four goals: to inform readers about current and future directions in teaching and learning in postsecondary education, to illuminate the context that shapes these new directions, to illustrate these new directions through examples from real settings, and to propose ways in which these new directions can be incorporated into still other settings.

This publication reflects the view that teaching deserves respect as a high form of scholarship. We believe that significant scholarship is conducted not only by researchers who report results of empirical investigations but also by practitioners who share disciplined reflections about teaching. Contributors to *NDTL* approach questions of teaching and learning as seriously as they approach substantive questions in their own disciplines, and they deal not only with pedagogical issues but also with the intellectual and social contexts in which these issues arise. Authors deal on the one hand with theory and research and on the other with practice, and they translate from research and theory to practice and back again.

*About This Volume.* The desire to continue a quest for multiculturalism in postsecondary education burns bright on campuses across the country. Just prior to the publication of this issue, new legal decisions have made it possible for institutions to once again pursue a diverse student population at public universities. As before, faculty and administrators are searching for new and effective ways of infusing multicultural instruction into the everyday life of the institution. This issue provides some very innovative suggestions to support their quest.

Marilla D. Svinicki
Editor-in-Chief

*MARILLA D. SVINICKI is associate professor of educational psychology at the University of Texas at Austin.*

# Editors' Notes

Because effective approaches to multicultural teaching and learning are still being developed in institutions across the United States and around the world, it is essential to study and document promising practices. It is only through rigorous research and comparative studies that we can be assured that the significant investments many institutions are making in multicultural education for the development of individual student and faculty skills and the overall betterment of society will yield positive results. This volume of *New Directions for Teaching and Learning* provides not only the valuable results of such research but also models for the types of research that others could carry out in this area.

That the current volume will appeal to instructors new to multicultural teaching who are looking for a guide to help map unfamiliar terrain should be clear. In ways less obvious but just as important, it should also meet the needs of those faculty who have devoted considerable time to these issues. Most U.S. campuses have some number of faculty, staff, and students who are committed activists for diversity and social justice, who find each other informally through coursework and cocurricular activities and organizations. In 2006, twelve professors at the University of Michigan who are known for their work in multicultural social justice were interviewed about the classes they teach to undergraduates. It is faculty such as these on whom many institutions rely for their multicultural and civically engaged offerings. Unfortunately, most of these faculty members said they often feel isolated from other colleagues who do social justice work. In addition, they report having no time or institutional position to formalize or design an interdisciplinary and integrated multicultural curriculum.

However, in order for institutions to reach many more students in effective and transformative ways, this work must be given a structure so that it is fully integrated into the curriculum. What we seek to offer in this volume are documented illustrations of how such learning is designed, carried out, and applied effectively across curricula and in a variety of higher education contexts. Such research and analysis offered here can then serve as a building block for larger curricular initiatives and reforms that go beyond the talents and motivations of extraordinary individual scholars and teachers.

Our authors' methods include surveys, analyses of class assignments, use of control and comparison groups, focus groups, interviews, standardized instruments, reflective writing, and long- and short-term outcomes. The items measured include skills and attitudes, knowledge and the development of new interests, commitments and insights, and measures of life

NEW DIRECTIONS FOR TEACHING AND LEARNING, no. 111, Fall 2007 © Wiley Periodicals, Inc.
Published online in Wiley InterScience (www.interscience.wiley.com) • DOI: 10.1002/tl.279

patterns, experiences, and demographics. The articles include some that are strongly based in cognitive or developmental theory, some that are directly testing hypotheses, and some that are based in action-research methods; a few include all three of these approaches.

The volume opens with Sue Kaufmann's overview of the current context of the retreat from affirmative action. We then look at faculty concerns and faculty development: Mark Chesler and Al Young examine faculty identity and its impact on teaching interactions, Suzanne Burgoyne and others explore best practices in using interactive theater for faculty multicultural pedagogical training, and Ilene Alexander describes effective resources for developing multicultural competence in future faculty. From there we turn to research on established multicultural strategies in chapters by Ratnesh Nagda and Pat Gurin on intergroup dialogues; Jo Paoletti, Eden Segal, and Christina Totino on service learning; and A. T. Miller and Edith Fernández on experiential field education. The remaining chapters present course-specific inquiries from engineering, by Cinda-Sue Davis and Cynthia Finelli; music performance, by Caroline Helton and Emery Stephens; information technology, by Eileen Trauth and others; political science, by Jeffery Bernstein; and mathematics, by Dale Winter. We thus examine a multitude of examples from across the curriculum using highly varied strategies to deliver multicultural content and investigate its impact.

We are indebted to the Carnegie Academy for the Scholarship of Teaching and Learning (CASTL) and the former American Association for Higher Education for sponsoring the CASTL Campus Program. As part of that effort we had the privilege of leading a cluster on the scholarship of multicultural teaching and learning, collaborating with colleagues from the Ohio State University, the Pennsylvania State University, the University of Iowa, the University of Minnesota, and the University of Missouri. This volume represents the final project of our cluster. We also thank our colleagues at the Center for Research on Learning and Teaching at the University of Michigan for their own ongoing commitment and efforts in this area, which continue to inform our work. We would like to offer special thanks to India McHale for her very timely and careful work preparing the manuscript for publication.

Matthew Kaplan
A. T. Miller
Editors

MATTHEW KAPLAN is managing director of the Center for Research on Learning and Teaching at the University of Michigan.

A. T. MILLER is coordinator of multicultural teaching and learning at the Center for Research on Learning and Teaching and director of the Global Intercultural Experiences for Undergraduates Program at the University of Michigan.

NEW DIRECTIONS FOR TEACHING AND LEARNING • DOI: 10.1002/tl

1

*As diversity increases in the general population, U.S. colleges and universities are struggling to maintain campus diversity in the context of legislative elimination of affirmative action in admissions.*

# The History and Impact of State Initiatives to Eliminate Affirmative Action

*Susan W. Kaufmann*

Since 1995, efforts to prohibit affirmative action have intensified, perhaps most strikingly in higher education. In 1996, California voters adopted Proposition 209 (Prop. 209), an amendment to the state constitution that banned both discrimination and affirmative action programs that give preferences to groups or individuals based on their race, gender, color, ethnicity, or national origin for public employment, education, or contracting purposes. Also in 1996, the Fifth Circuit Court of Appeals issued a decision, *Hopwood* v. *Texas*, ending affirmative action in private and public college and university admissions in Texas, Louisiana, and Mississippi. Late in 1997, *Gratz* v. *Bollinger* and *Grutter* v. *Bollinger* challenged the use of affirmative action in undergraduate and law school admissions, respectively. In 1998, Washington voters passed Initiative 200 (I-200), nearly identical to Prop. 209 except a state law, not a constitutional amendment. In 1999, Florida Governor Jeb Bush preissued an executive order ending consideration of race and ethnicity in public college and university admissions, public employment, and government contracting.

In 2003, the U.S. Supreme Court, in both *Grutter* v. *Bollinger* and *Gratz* v. *Bollinger,* affirmed the validity of race-based affirmative action in college admissions. During a holistic review of each applicant's strengths and potential contributions to the class, the Court concluded, race or ethnicity could be considered as one factor among many others, if it is not done

NEW DIRECTIONS FOR TEACHING AND LEARNING, no. 111, Fall 2007  © Wiley Periodicals, Inc.
Published online in Wiley InterScience (www.interscience.wiley.com) • DOI: 10.1002/tl.280

mechanistically. A variety of evidence persuaded the Supreme Court to uphold affirmative action:

- Students of *all* races who live and learn among diverse peers in both formal classroom and informal settings that challenge them to absorb and respond to new points of view develop the capacity for more original and critical thinking. They also develop "democracy skills, including greater tolerance for differences as a normal part of life" (Gurin, 1997; Gurin, Dey, Hurtado, and Gurin, 2002, p. 330).
- "Race unfortunately still matters" in American life, as evidenced by continuing disparities ("Brief," 2003, p. 23).
- "The path to leadership must be visibly open to talented and qualified individuals of every race and ethnicity" ("Brief," 2003, p. 23).
- Over three hundred organizations filed amicus (friend of the court) briefs on behalf of the University of Michigan, the largest number ever filed in a case before the Supreme Court.

The Court found particularly persuasive the military's amicus brief, which stated that the armed forces could not assemble a diverse officer corps without employing affirmative action in the military academies, and it could not lead effectively—or even safely—if officers did not reflect the diversity of the enlistees, making affirmative action a matter of national security ("Brief," 2003, p. 22). The brief filed by sixty-five *Fortune* 500 businesses similarly emphasized the centrality of affirmative action to their core values and operations, asserting that "an educational environment that ensures participation by diverse people, viewpoints and ideas will help produce the most talented workforce" ("Brief," 2003, pp. 1–2).

Two weeks after the Supreme Court issued its decisions in the *Grutter* and *Gratz* cases, *Gratz* plaintiff Jennifer Gratz and Ward Connerly launched a Michigan ballot initiative campaign. Called the Michigan Civil Rights Initiative, or Proposal 2, the measure—a constitutional amendment virtually identical to Prop. 209—passed in 2006. Following that victory, Connerly and Gratz announced that they are exploring the feasibility of mounting campaigns in several western states. Ironically, efforts to end affirmative action are occurring during a period of rapid demographic change in the United States. U.S. Census Bureau data for 2005 show that non-Hispanic whites are now a minority in four states, including Texas and California.

## Impact of Prop. 209 on Higher Education in California

Passing a ballot initiative is only the first step in determining its policy implications; often courts must interpret the language so that policy decisions can be made. In September 1997, California Governor Pete Wilson held a press conference to announce a list of over thirty "offending statutes" that he believed violated Prop. 209 and called on the legislature to repeal or amend them (California Governor's Office, 1997). These statutes included precollege outreach and preparation programs, scholarships and fellowships, and professional training programs. Subsequently, references to race and gender in those California programs have been either eliminated or replaced by socioeconomic status, a highly problematic proxy for race since not all underrepresented minorities have low incomes and even those who are affluent may still experience bias and discrimination.

## Impact of Prop. 209 on University Enrollments at the University of California

According to Richard Atkinson, former president of the University of California system, "In 1995, before Proposition 209 took effect, underrepresented minority students accounted for 38 percent of California high school graduates and 21 percent of entering University of California freshmen, a difference of 17 percent. In 2004, they made up 45 percent of high school graduates but had fallen to 18 percent of incoming UC freshmen, a difference of 27 percent" (Atkinson and Pelfrey, 2005, p. 8). Enrollment decreases at UC Berkeley and UCLA have been even steeper. Atkinson continues, "In 1995, UC Berkeley and UCLA together enrolled a total of 469 African-American women and men in a combined freshman class of 7,100. In 2004, the number was 218, out of a combined freshman class of 7,350. African-American men, in particular, are virtually disappearing from our campuses. UCLA and Berkeley together admitted 83 African-American men in 2004" (p. 8). In 2006, UCLA, which is located in the county with the second largest African American population in the United States ("Struggling," 2006), enrolled the smallest number of entering African American freshmen "since at least 1973" (Trounson, 2006, p. 1).

The percentage of Latino students attending the University of California also dropped following passage of Prop. 209. Although the trend reversed in 2001 and the percentage of Latino students admitted to the University of California system now exceeds pre–Prop. 209 levels, it does so in the context of a rapidly increasing Latino population in the state of California. The percentage of Latinos at Berkeley and UCLA is still significantly lower than in 1997. The percentage of Native American students enrolled in the UC system dropped 38 percent from 1997 to 2006 and has not been increasing (University of California, 2006).

Low and declining enrollments of underrepresented minority students at the University of California follow several changes resulting from Prop. 209: the end of affirmative action (Birgeneau, 2005a; 2005b); elimination of targeted outreach programs (Laird, 2005); the perception, as their numbers dwindle, that the university is unwelcoming to underrepresented minorities (Birgeneau, 2005a); and a growing tendency for underrepresented students with strong academic records to enroll elsewhere (Laird, 2005). These Prop. 209–related trends are occurring in the context of

NEW DIRECTIONS FOR TEACHING AND LEARNING • DOI: 10.1002/tl

"disparities in [K–12] educational opportunity for underrepresented students," including access to Advanced Placement and honors curricula (Contreras, 2005); reduction or elimination of state funding for race-neutral college preparatory and outreach programs (Torres, 2004); increasing competition and selectivity in University of California admissions as applications rise faster than capacity (Laird, 2005; Rendón, Novack, and Dowell, 2005); and rising tuition (Laird, 2005) and decreasing need-based financial aid (Kidder, Serrano, and Acheta, 2004). The fact that UC Berkeley typically receives more than twice as many applications from students with grades above 4.0 as it has places in the freshman class is one measure of the intense competition for admission (Laird, 2005).

The University of California has tried many race-neutral means of increasing enrollments of underrepresented students since affirmative action became illegal (Atkinson and Pelfrey, 2005, pp. 6–8):

- Outreach programs to high schools that send few students to the University of California
- Emphasis on achievement rather than aptitude tests
- Comprehensive review of applications, including consideration of obstacles students have overcome and the use they have made of opportunities
- Eligibility under the Local Context Project, a percentage plan making students graduating in the top 4 percent of each high school eligible for enrollment at one of the University of California campuses, provided they have taken a series of required courses
- Guaranteed admission to a University of California campus for community college transfer students meeting course and grade requirements

According to Atkinson and Pelfrey (2005), "Despite enormous efforts, we have failed badly to achieve the goal of a student body that encompasses California's diverse population. . . . Any state tempted to emulate the example of California should think long and hard about the consequences" (p. 10). For UC Berkeley Chancellor Robert Birgeneau, diversity is the foundation of effective education: "We are . . . missing out on exceptional African American, Latino and Native American students who can not only succeed here, but whose participation can improve the education the university offers all its students. . . . The single most important skill that a 21st century student must master is 'intercultural competence'—the ability . . . to navigate successfully in today's globalized society" (2005a).

## Impact of Prop. 209 on University Enrollments at the California State University

Enrollments of African Americans and Native Americans have also fallen at the California State University as a percentage of total enrollments since the passage of Prop. 209. In 1996 and 1997, African American enrollment

NEW DIRECTIONS FOR TEACHING AND LEARNING • DOI: 10.1002/tl

peaked at 7.3 percent of the total. Beginning in 1998, it declined each year, reaching 6.5 percent in 2004, an 11 percent decrease. Native American enrollment peaked at 1.2 percent from 1994 to 1996 and dropped steadily to 0.8 percent in 2004, a 25 percent decrease (Schreck, 2006). Rapidly rising enrollment pressure from the children of the baby boomers means that admission to California State campuses is becoming increasingly competitive and beginning to be affected by many of the same forces shaping University of California enrollments (Rendón, Novack, and Dowell, 2005).

## Percentage Plans

California, Texas, and Florida have all mandated "percentage plans" to replace affirmative action. Those plans require that students who rank in a specified top percentage of their high school graduating class be admitted to a campus in the state university system. Although the plans have had limited success in broadening access, typically by rural students (Laird, 2005), they have not generally succeeded in maintaining the level of student body diversity achieved with affirmative action (Tienda and others, 2003), particularly on the most competitive campuses (Horn and Flores, 2003). For one thing, many students eligible under percentage plans would already have been eligible under existing admissions criteria (Laird, 2005; Horn and Flores, 2003). In addition, such plans have required massive and expensive new outreach programs, along with large infusions of scholarship support (Tienda and others, 2003), to encourage top-performing students in schools that rarely send students to universities to apply and attend. Furthermore, the plans' success in achieving diversity depends largely on existing segregation in the states' school systems (Laird, 2005). Following the *Grutter* decision, the University of Texas at Austin has reinstated affirmative action alongside its percentage plan (Laird, 2005).

## Conclusion

Eliminating affirmative action in California has led to a number of consequences in the educational realm: declining percentages of underrepresented minorities enrolled at the University of California, especially at flagship institutions, as well as at the California State University; the end of targeted outreach efforts; and the failure of alternative methods, including a percentage plan, to maintain the level of diversity achieved under affirmative action. In addition to the impact of undergraduate student enrollment covered in this chapter, these efforts have also led to significant decreases in graduate and professional school enrollment of underrepresented students, decreases in the hiring of women faculty and faculty of color at the University of California, and the elimination of voluntary school desegregation efforts in some cities, with continuing challenges in others.

As the U.S. Supreme Court noted in *Grutter* v. *Bollinger,* students of all races who experience the benefits and challenges of living and learning among diverse peers develop the capacity for more original and critical thinking. They also develop the ability to negotiate both difference and commonality within and between groups. Years after graduating, students who have learned to engage effectively with members of other groups in college remain more likely to maintain cross-racial relationships and to live in integrated communities. Such experience is particularly important because most students, particularly whites, grow up in segregated communities and experience diversity for the first time when they go to college (Atkinson and Pelfrey, 2005; Gurin, 1997; Gurin, Dey, Hurtado, and Gurin, 2002). In addition, employers value students educated in highly diverse educational settings because they are better able to integrate different perspectives to solve problems, develop and market products that appeal to a variety of customers, partner with constituencies in the United States and around the world, and discourage discrimination and stereotyping ("Brief," 2003). Since the passage of Prop. 209, opportunities for students in California public universities to learn among peers who reflect the diversity of the state and to derive the benefits of such an education have diminished, particularly the most selective institutions.

Ten years after Prop. 209, its effects continue to unfold. To varying degrees, similar trends have resulted from affirmative action bans in Washington, Florida, and Texas. Now Michigan institutions and policymakers, aware of consequences elsewhere, are searching for ways to preserve diversity within the framework of Proposal 2, while Ward Connerly and Jennifer Gratz are planning a multistate effort to pass additional referendums in the hope that the U.S. Supreme Court will eventually abolish affirmative action.

## References

Atkinson, R., and Pelfrey, A. "Opportunity in a Democratic Society: A National Agenda." Paper prepared for the Third Annual Nancy Cantor Distinguished Lecture on Intellectual Diversity, delivered by Richard C. Atkinson at the University of Michigan, May 18, 2005.

Birgeneau, R. J. "Anti-Bias Law Has Backfired at Berkeley." UC Berkeley Web Feature. Mar. 29, 2005a. http://www.berkeley.edu/news/media/releases/2005/03/29_oped. shtml. Accessed Nov. 28, 2005.

Birgeneau, R. J. "'The System Is Broken': Chancellor Robert J. Birgeneau Discusses Proposition 209 and Its Consequences at UC Berkeley." UC Berkeley Web Feature. Mar. 29, 2005b. http://www.berkeley.edu/news/media/releases/2005/03/29_birgeneau. shtml. Accessed Nov. 28, 2005.

"Brief for Amici Curiae 65 Leading American Businesses in Support of Respondents," In *Grutter et al.* v. *Bollinger et al.,* 539 U.S. 306 (2003), Feb. 18, 2003.

California Governor's Office. "Wilson Unveils List of 30 Offending Statutes." Press Release 97:331. Sept. 9, 1997. http://aad.english.ucsb.edu/docs/wilson.9-97.html. Accessed May 22, 2007.

Contreras, F. E. "The Reconstruction of Merit Post–Proposition 209." *Educational Policy,* 2005, *19*(2), 371–395.

Gurin, P. "Expert Report of Patricia Gurin." In *The Compelling Need for Diversity in Higher Education*. Ann Arbor: University of Michigan, 1997. http://www.vpcomm. umich.edu/admissions/legal/expert/gurintoc.html. Accessed May 22, 2007.

Gurin, P., Dey, E., Hurtado, S., and Gurin, G. "Diversity and Higher Education: Theory and Impact on Educational Outcomes." *Harvard Educational Review*, 2002, 72(3), 330–366.

Horn, C., and Flores, S. *Percent Plans in College Admissions: A Comparative Analysis of Three States' Experience*. Cambridge, Mass.: Civil Rights Project, Harvard University, 2003.

Kidder, W., Serrano, S. K., and Acheta, A. N. "In California, a Misguided Battle over Race." *Chronicle of Higher Education*, 2004, 50(37), p. B16. http://chronicle.com/prm/ weekly/v50/i37/37b01601.htm. Accessed May 22, 2007.

Laird, B. *The Case for Affirmative Action in University Admissions*. Berkeley, Calif.: Bay Tree, 2005.

Rendón, L. I., Novack, V., and Dowell, D. "Testing Race-Neutral Admission Models: Lessons from California State University–Long Beach." *Review of Higher Education*, 2005, 28(2), 221–243.

Schreck, A. "Changing Faces of California State University Faculty and Students: A Summary of Data on the Racial/Ethnic and Gender Diversity in the CSU." Paper presented at the CFA Equity Conference 2006: Building Power Through Diversity and Activism, Mar. 2006.

"Struggling to Keep Black Students." *Inside Higher Ed*, June 6, 2006, citing Darnell Hunt, head of the Ralph Bunche Center for African American Studies, UCLA. http://inside-highered.com/layout/set/print/news/2006/06/06/black. Accessed June 6, 2006.

Tienda, M., Leicht, K. T., Sullivan, T., Maltese, M., and Lloyd, K. "Closing the Gap? Admissions and Enrollments at the Texas Public Flagships Before and After Affirmative Action." Working Paper no. 2003-01. Princeton, N.J.: Office of Population Research, Princeton University, 2003.

Torres, C. "Eliminating Outreach at the University of California: Program Contributions and the Consequences of Their Reductions." Los Angeles: Tomas Rivera Policy Institute, University of Southern California, 2004.

Trounson, R. "A Startling Statistic at UCLA." *Los Angeles Times*, June 3, 2006, p. 1. http://www.latimes.com/news/printedition/front/la-me-ucla3jun03. Accessed June 5, 2006.

University of California. "Table 2. Distribution of Statement of Intent to Register (SIRs) for Admitted Freshmen, Fall 1997 Through 2006." May 31, 2006. http://www.ucop. edu/news/factsheets/2006/froshsirs_table2.pdf. Accessed May 22, 2007.

*SUSAN W. KAUFMANN is the associate director for advocacy of the University of Michigan Center for the Education of Women.*

# 2

*How do faculty members' social group identities influence their choices about how they present themselves and their course materials? How do these identities affect student responses to them and the material they present?*

# Faculty Members' Social Identities and Classroom Authority

*Mark Chesler, Alford A. Young Jr.*

Social group identity is as relevant to the teaching-learning enterprise as it is to thought and behavior in all other walks of life. Membership in social groups identifiable by race or ethnicity, gender, age, and other characteristics affects the ways in which we think and act and the ways in which others perceive us, act toward us, and react to us. Specifically, we know that faculty members with different social group identities experience the academy differently and have varied reactions to those experiences. Several major studies and a number of first-person anthologies testify to different rates of representation, status or rank, level of satisfaction, approaches to the classroom and curriculum, encounters with students, and relationships with colleagues (Adams, Bell, and Griffin, 1997; Banks and Banks, 1995; Castellanos and Jones, 2003; Dews and Law, 1995; Hune, 1998; Li and Beckett, 2006; Lim and Herrera-Sobek, 2000; Macdonald and Sánchez-Casal, 2002; Maher and Tetrault, 1994; Mayberry, 1996; Padilla and Chavez, 1995; Stanley, 2006a; Turner and Myers, 2000; Valian, 1998; Vargas, 2002). Overall, the power of whiteness and maleness as identities privileged by academic institutions' cultures and structures provides the context within which individual faculty members encounter and respond to diverse students and their actions in and out of the classroom.

In this chapter we examine how the social group identities of faculty members are reflected in their pedagogical encounters and practices. More particularly, we consider how faculty members with different social group

NEW DIRECTIONS FOR TEACHING AND LEARNING, no. 111, Fall 2007 © Wiley Periodicals, Inc.
Published online in Wiley InterScience (www.interscience.wiley.com) • DOI: 10.1002/tl.281

identities deal with two issues commonly faced by all faculty: questions about their subject matter expertise and questions about the authority of the faculty role. Both areas are often the grounds on which students covertly or overtly challenge faculty authority.

In exploring these issues we conducted face-to-face interviews with a sample of 64 faculty members at a major midwestern research extensive university. A diverse sample (by race or ethnicity, gender, and discipline) of faculty was recruited for these interviews (32 females and 32 males; 18 whites, 20 African Americans, 13 Asian Americans, 9 Latinos and Latinas, and 4 Native Americans; 25 social scientists, 22 natural scientists, and 17 humanists). Faculty were selected on the basis of their local reputations as outstanding instructors and as especially thoughtful practitioners of teaching in diverse classrooms. Thus no attempt was made to gather a representative sample; rather, the aim was to solicit the most advanced thinking and experience on these issues from what is in many ways a particularly sophisticated cadre. Many of these individuals have won teaching awards, and all express a commitment not just to teaching but to teaching effectively in a diverse environment. As result, these faculty may be more aware of, sensitive to, and adept at dealing with these issues than their colleagues.

The excerpts presented here reflect faculty members' own perceptions and interpretations—not those of their students and colleagues—as received, organized, and interpreted by the authors.

## Assuming, Asserting, and Dealing with Academic Expertise and Challenges to It

As the dominant face of the faculty, white and male faculty members can make—and can assume that students will make—assumptions about the high level of their subject matter expertise. Very few of the white faculty interviewed anticipated or encountered a challenge to their expertise. Indeed, when faced with the occasional student challenge, one white male faculty member indicated that he felt he could afford to be challenged and even to make mistakes: "I can make errors; I can make mistakes; I can have a bad day; I can be disorganized; I can use terms incorrectly; and most faculty of color cannot."

Other tenured white faculty also expressed relative comfort in addressing perceived or potential conflicts with students over course material. As one white female colleague who teaches about race and ethnicity stated, "I have a lot of authority in the classroom, but I also create an atmosphere so that if students are unhappy, they feel completely at ease to tell me they're unhappy. . . . I don't think that if I was a male, I would get students coming at me. But I've definitely had conflicts over authority, conflicts with men in the classroom. I learned a lot from that stuff." Thus while acknowledging conflict and potential challenge and their relation to her gender, this white colleague also indicates that she knows how to deal with their occurrence with relative comfort.

NEW DIRECTIONS FOR TEACHING AND LEARNING • DOI: 10.1002/tl

The tension and anxieties experienced by faculty of color were not so easily resolved or managed. In part, this is due to the social reality that upon standing in the front of a classroom, these faculty immediately and starkly became visible examples of difference for their students. For instance, two African American male natural scientists discussed their experiences as follows. One confided, "In a sense, I lack a kind of authority. There are certain students that I have to prove myself to. There are students who I think are not prepared to accept me as an authority on the subject matter, whether it's because of my race or my politics." The other noted, "When I walk into the classroom, my anticipation is that I will be challenged; that's why I've got to be prepared, and I think that with that philosophy it's easier for me to be well prepared because I expect and anticipate, you know, the worst." The first colleague's statement reflects the dilemma, common to faculty of color, of knowing that his expertise is questioned by students but not knowing clearly whether that is a function of his race or other aspects of his persona. The second colleague clearly expresses the anticipatory vigilance and even sense of dread accompanying his entry into a challenging and potentially disconfirming environment.

Purwar (2004) argues that "authority is seen to be especially misplaced when it is clearly vested in a woman of color" (p. 52), and several female faculty members of color reported their experiences in this regard. In one case, an Asian American colleague discussed the relatively narrow grounds on which she expected her expertise to be accepted by students: "I also think that if students know, for example, that I do Asian American studies . . . , then somehow they perceive me as less able to talk about a range of other issues. So they would perceive that I don't know how to read white scholars. Or that whenever we do read white scholars, you can sense this little surprise, like, 'Oh, she can do that too.'"

An African American female social scientist reported that she acted very early in the semester to avoid or neutralize potential challenges to her expertise: "I do my background routine. I tell them I have these degrees. . . . 'I may be the first black face you've ever seen, but there are a lot of us with Ph.D.'s, and I have one.' It's totally mind-boggling for some folks." This colleague is aware of her anticipation of being challenged by students and takes steps to prevent or foreclose it. Her prior experience with challenge and ensuing personal discomfort or classroom disruption has led her to respond by getting her credentials on the table at the outset.

With experience, and with the added weight of age, some of these challenges to expertise may recede or become easier to deal with—at least, that was the perspective of a female African American natural scientist, who said, "It's a little different now that I've got a little more maturity and a few gray hairs. . . . It was most challenging when [I was] green, just starting, and it's easy for students to kind of dismiss faculty of color, if they see that there are other ways to get the information, or to discount your knowledge and your experience." Younger faculty, younger female faculty, younger faculty of color, and especially younger female faculty of color consistently report more challenges to their substantive expertise and more pain and discomfort (sometimes anger as well) in dealing with those challenges.

The foregoing comments demonstrate that challenges to a faculty member's standing as a subject matter expert can occur to anyone, regardless of race, gender, or seniority. However, the racial, gender, and seniority status of professors directly affects the degree to which they are challenged about what or how much they know about their topic and the manner in which they interpret and respond to such challenges (including whether they feel inclined or obliged to respond at all).

## Dealing with Institutional Role and Authority and Challenges to Them

The same pattern holds regarding faculty members' differential assessments of how they deal with challenges to their role and authority status in the classroom. Faculty who possess social identity characteristics that are not privileged spoke of having to force recognition of their professional role and the deference that faculty generally believe should accompany it. For instance, in assessing her experiences and struggles in comparison to other professors in the university classroom, a white female colleague stressed the importance of gender: "I think men have it way too easy in the classroom. They don't have a clue how much harder it is to have authority and to get respect and to just not have to deal with a lot of bull—from some students." Another white female natural science scholar said, "I can't get away with saying things like 'Shut up' [because] there are huge gender differences in what students expect of a teacher. They would not call a male instructor on that. But they would call a woman on that. If a woman did that, there'd be immediate complaints that would affect the whole semester." She went on to report that students' preconceived notions of gender roles can influence their expectations of faculty and their perceptions of whether faculty members are meeting these expectations: "I cotaught with a male one semester—he had no office hours, [and] he answered no e-mails. He did teach the class. [Yet at the end of the semester,] he got higher scores on accessibility [and] on evaluations than I did! I had office hours even when he was lecturing. I answered every e-mail. The students came to my office hours. My accessibility score was lower. And that's a difference in expectation."

These perceptions of accessibility and the character of student-faculty interpersonal relationships are exacerbated when less privileged racial and gender statuses are in play. As one Latina scholar said, "Different faculty take certain hierarchical positions which affect the whole question of what they're supposed to call me—Professor XXX, my first name, or whatever. It has everything to do with how old I am, my gender, my race. The reality is

I'd prefer if they'd call me Professor XXX. But they don't usually. They call me by my first name."

A second female faculty of color indicated how she more directly addressed such actual as well as potential challenges to her status and how some students tried to relate with her. In one instance, a student left a message after hours on her answering machine stating that she planned to join the class and demanding that the faculty member call her back to specify the readings for the next day. "And why would she think that I would be around to just pick up the phone? Because people do assume, particularly with African American women, that we are their 'mamas,' and some of them go so far as to say things like that. And I say, 'I'm a warm person, I'm a kind person. . . . I know this may be the first black woman you've interacted with except your maid, but I'm not your maid.'" She planned to have a face-to-face encounter with this student, a strategy she uses regularly to address such challenges to her authority. Among the key dilemmas reported are the tension between authority and warmth or kindness and the ways in which accessibility, warmth, or innovation by female scholars and scholars of color may be interpreted and reacted to by students as signs of weakness or loss of traditional forms of authority.

It is important to note that some faculty of color indicated that challenges to their status and authority did not come exclusively from white students. As one African American woman said in discussing the consequences of bringing her personal experiences into the classroom, "I've had students [of color] after class come up to me and hug me, I'm not a touchy-feely person. . . . It makes me very uncomfortable. I think they mean it positively, but I also wonder if they mean it as, 'Well, we're both black, and there's some connection.' So . . . I simply say, 'I'm not unreasonable, [but] look, I'm your teacher; you're my student; we're not friends.'"

These cases demonstrate that challenges to a faculty member's institutional role or authority status do not have to take the form of aggressive or pernicious interactions. Alternatively, challenges can take the form of students' trying to reposition faculty members as fulfilling supportive, nurturing, or intimate roles rather than professional ones. This is done, or at least expected, precisely because such faculty members stand in social identity categories that have not been traditionally associated with faculty status in the academy.

Another African American female scholar explained her own way of dealing with these issues by indicating that she forthrightly asserted and maintained a position of authority. She said, "The first thing is to set the tone in the first class session that you are in charge. Don't ever let that slip, because the moment you do, because you are a person of color, you will never regain that. It's a cliché that to a certain extent that if you are a person of color you have to come doubly prepared, because you will get challenges in classroom settings that your peers simply won't ever great."

In pulling together the effects of race or ethnicity and gender on challenges to institutional authority and how this can be handled (at least to some extent), a female scholar of color explained that appearance mattered as much as conduct in her effort to establish her authority in the classroom: "How can a nonwhite woman assert authoritativeness in a classroom dominated by white males for whom authority figures have been largely other white males? . . . Attire is a big part of it. I'm always conscious of how I dress on teaching days."

These comments contrast with the sentiment of a senior African American male professor who explained with relative ease how he functions in his classroom and how that compared with what he believes female faculty of color have to confront in that setting: "I let the students start off. And so long as I can get them where I want them to go without telling them, you get the same result each time, but never the same route. And that's easy, see; that's fun. . . . And when I mention this to younger colleagues . . . , especially black women, [they] can't fathom going into a classroom that way. Because . . . they're concerned that their authority will be undermined. They say, 'You're male and you're older.'"

In a comment that further clarifies what the differences in respect and deference to authority often are for white scholars and scholars of color and how race, gender, and age operate simultaneously in this circumstance, an Asian American female scholar said the following:

> I always admired professors who were kind of older—senior men usually. . . . They have a lot more authority, but also they're able to be kinder in the classroom or to be more generous to their students. . . . Whereas I'm kind of a small person, right? And a woman and Asian, right? So it's almost the opposite of the ideal teacher. So I would like to be kind and generous and be perceived to be that way. But often I feel like the only way that I can do that is if I appear very old as a way to kind of offset those things.

These comments demonstrate that mastery of course content is far from all that is necessary to ensure that faculty of color and female faculty secure the kind of respect and deference that is accorded to higher education faculty who occupy more privileged identity categories. Aside from matters concerning the depth or extent of a professor's scholarly expertise, there remains the issue of what it means for professors to appear in front of a classroom in possession of bodies that do not match the image that many students associate with the professoriate.

## Discussion and Implications

The ultimate pedagogical dilemma for faculty who face this situation, then, is to work at ensuring and preserving the authority that has a place in relationships with students while also maintaining a healthy and vibrant educational climate. Moreover, they may wonder whether they really are being challenged more often than white males, whether those they do face are imbued with more intensity or hostility, or whether they are simply more sensitive to challenges that do occur.

White male (and senior) faculty who do not encounter the same challenges or who do not interpret or react to them in the same way may be puzzled by these reports from female colleagues and colleagues of color and not know how to deal with them. It may seem as though faculty in subordinate categories are less competent or that they imagine these problems or create them themselves. However, the situation requires that white and male peers and administrators understand that these challenges emerge in very different ways and potencies for different kinds of faculty.

Where does one go for help and support in dealing with such challenges? What would help? Particularly good resources for a wide range of answers to these questions can be found in Moody (2004) and Stanley (2006b). But in the midst of a culture of assumed expertise and surrounded by a generally lower priority of teaching in general, let alone teaching competently in a diverse classroom, advice, assistance, and support may be hard to come by at the local level. Most young faculty receive little instruction or mentoring about teaching and none at all about the unique ways in which the social identities of faculty and students may play out in the classroom.

Workshops and faculty development programs for graduate students and young faculty may help some of the abstract information about managing one's expertise and role become concrete and realistic. Then female faculty and faculty of color may anticipate some of the relatively unique issues they will face and can plan their approaches to the classroom and their responses to potential challenges. Cadres of female faculty and faculty of color can be encouraged to meet and share their experiences and approaches with one another. It is crucial for these faculty members, above all, to be true to themselves and to find ways of teaching and of meeting the challenges of teaching that reflect their own personal and cultural styles and priorities. For some that may mean facing such challenges directly and pointing out to students the racial and gender assumptions underlying their responses; for others it may mean avoiding direct engagement and focusing on traditional instructional content and pedagogies.

And some attention must be paid to students and the expectations they bring into the diverse collegiate environment. Orientation programs may help prepare students to anticipate, recognize, and deal with their own and their peers' often implicit or subconscious perceptions and biases of faculty members of diverse backgrounds.

In addition, discussions with senior white and male faculty can provide an opportunity to share the wisdom of experience and help establish greater understanding of the particular issues that female faculty and faculty of color are likely to encounter, including the potential impact of race and

NEW DIRECTIONS FOR TEACHING AND LEARNING • DOI: 10.1002/tl

gender status on student ratings of faculty (see Basow, 1998; Kardia and Wright, 2004). Members of more privileged groups may then take some responsibility for establishing a departmental or collegiate culture of respect and mutual support that makes life easier for all faculty. As long as the academy remains a white and male hegemonic site, nothing less than major efforts at culture change will fundamentally address the inequities faced by female faculty and faculty of color. The classroom and the academy itself are creatures of the larger society, and all the broader struggles around affirmative action and race and gender in higher education constitute background for the issues discussed in this chapter.

## References

Adams, M., Bell, L. A., and Griffin, P. (eds.). *Teaching for Diversity and Social Justice: A Sourcebook*. New York: Routledge, 1997.

Banks, J. A., and Banks, C.A.M. (eds.). *Handbook of Research on Multicultural Education*. Old Tappan, N.J.: Macmillan, 1995.

Basow, S. A. "Student Evaluations: Gender Bias and Teaching Styles." In L. H. Collins, J. C. Chrisler, and K. Quina (eds.). *Career Strategies for Women in Academe: Arming Athena*. Thousand Oaks, Calif.: Sage, 1998.

Castellanos, J., and Jones, L. (eds.). *The Majority in the Minority: Expanding the Representation of Latina/o Faculty, Administrators and Students in Higher Education*. Sterling, Va.: Stylus, 2003.

Dews, C.L.B., and Law, C. L. (eds.). *This Fine Place So Far from Home: Voices of Academics from the Working Class*. Philadelphia: Temple University Press, 1995.

Hune, S. *Asian Pacific American Women in Higher Education: Claiming Visibility and Voice*. Washington, D.C.: Association of American Colleges and Universities, 1998.

Kardia, D. B., and Wright, M. C. "Instructor Identity: The Impact of Gender and Race on Faculty Experiences with Teaching." CRLT Occasional Papers no. 19. Ann Arbor: University of Michigan Center for Research on Learning and Teaching, 2004.

Li, G., and Beckett, G. H. (eds.). *Strangers in the Academy: Asian Women Scholars in Higher Education*. Sterling, Va.: Stylus, 2006.

Lim, S., and Herrera-Sobek, M. (eds.). *Power, Race, and Gender in Academe: Strangers in the Tower*. New York: Modern Language Association of America, 2000.

Macdonald, A. A., and Sánchez-Casal, S. (eds.). *Twenty-First-Century Feminist Classrooms*. New York: Palgrave Macmillan, 2002.

Maher, F. A., and Tetrault, M.K.T. *The Feminist Classroom: Dynamics of Gender, Race, and Privilege*. New York: Basic Books, 1994.

Mayberry, K. J. (ed.). *Teaching What You Are Not: Identity Politics in Higher Education*. New York: New York University Press, 1996.

Moody, J. *Faculty Diversity: Problems and Solutions*. New York: Routledge, 2004.

Padilla, R. V., and Chavez, R. C. (eds.). *The Leaning Ivory Tower: Latino Professors in American Universities*. New York: State University of New York Press, 1995.

Purwar, N. "Fish in or out of Water: A Theoretical Framework for Race and the Space of Academia." In I. Law, D. Phillips, and L. Turney (eds.), *Institutional Racism in Higher Education*. Sterling, Va.: Trentham Books, 2004.

Stanley, C. A. (ed.). *Faculty of Color Teaching in Predominantly White Colleges and Universities*. Bolton, Mass.: Anker, 2006a.

Stanley, C. A. "Summary and Key Recommendations for the Recruitment and Retention of Faculty of Color." In C. Stanley (ed.), *Faculty of Color Teaching in Predominantly White Colleges and Universities*. Bolton, Mass.: Anker, 2006b.

Turner, C.S.V., and Myers, S. L., Jr. *Faculty of Color in Academe: Bittersweet Success.* Boston: Allyn & Bacon, 2000.

Valian, V. *Why So Slow? The Advancement of Women.* Cambridge, Mass.: MIT Press, 1998.

Vargas, L. (ed.). *Women Faculty of Color in the White Classroom: Narratives on the Pedagogical Implications of Classroom Diversity.* New York: Lang, 2002.

*MARK CHESLER is emeritus professor of sociology at the University of Michigan.*

*ALFORD A. YOUNG JR. is associate professor of sociology and Afroamerican and African studies at the University of Michigan.*

NEW DIRECTIONS FOR TEACHING AND LEARNING • DOI: 10.1002/tl

# 3

*What are the advantages and drawbacks of using inter-active theater for faculty development on multicultural issues?*

# Interactive Theater and Self-Efficacy

*Suzanne Burgoyne, Peggy Placier, Mallory Thomas, Sharon Welch, Clyde Ruffin, Lisa Y. Flores, Elif Celebi, Noor Azizan-Gardner, Marilyn Miller*

*"Stop!"* A faculty member interrupts the performance. She comes onstage to replace the actor playing the professor of Statistics 101, to try out her own strategy for turning a student argument about diversity into a "teachable moment." This is forum theater, an interactive theater method in which audience members become active performers, taking advantage of the opportunity to explore multicultural dimensions of teaching in a "safe space" and get feedback from colleagues.

When the University of Missouri-Columbia (Mizzou) joined the Carnegie cluster on the Scholarship of Multicultural Teaching and Learning, our interdisciplinary campus team had already been investigating inter-active theater as pedagogy (see, for example, Burgoyne, 2002, and Placier and others, 2005). Forum theater methods derive from Theater of the Oppressed, an interactive approach founded by the Brazilian Augusto Boal, drawing on Paolo Freire's "pedagogy of the oppressed" (1970).

Borrowing a script written by Jeffrey Steiger, artistic director of the theater program at the University of Michigan's Center for Research on Learning and Teaching (CRLT), which depicts a classroom conflict sparked by multi-cultural issues, we performed for faculty and graduate teaching assistants. Up to a point, our performances followed Michigan's model: a short sketch followed by audience discussion with the characters.

The interactive theater approach includes a number of alternative methods; discussion with characters may lead to a general discussion of

NEW DIRECTIONS FOR TEACHING AND LEARNING, no. 111, Fall 2007 © Wiley Periodicals, Inc.
Published online in Wiley InterScience (www.interscience.wiley.com) • DOI: 10.1002/tl.282

teaching strategies to address the situation; audience feedback followed by the actors' replay of the sketch, with the instructor-character using strategies suggested by the audience; or the forum theater method, in which an audience member comes onstage either to replace the instructor or as an additional character. While Michigan's CRLT theater program has explored a number of different approaches, Mizzou's project focused on the forum theater method, with spectators replacing the instructor and trying out their ideas while the actors improvise realistic responses. CRLT staff members, particularly Steiger, provided valuable advice and suggestions as we developed Mizzou's forum theater project.

## The Study

Although practitioners all over the world apply forum theater, little empirical research has examined the use of these techniques for enhancing teacher effectiveness. Most existing literature on Theater of the Oppressed consists primarily of case studies, ideological analyses, and interviews with Boal (see, for instance, Schutzman and Cohen-Cruz, 1994).

We used qualitative methods to assess the forum theater performance's impact. Our grounded theory analysis of focus group and follow-up e-mail survey data yielded similar results to Michigan's study of interactive performances on its campus: participants found the active learning approach memorable, increasing "audience awareness of key issues" (Kaplan, Cook, and Steiger, 2006, p. 34). Mizzou's grounded theory study, which will be published in full elsewhere, also suggests that a complex interweaving of audience members' individual background and assumptions, including assumptions about the role of the professor in the classroom, may affect their reactions to the performance and the impact it has on them as teachers.

Participants in our first focus group (FG1), for instance, impressed us with the emotional intensity of their resistance to dealing with diversity in the classroom. They argued that their disciplines hadn't prepared them, they just wanted to teach content, and trying to cope with student difference would drive them crazy. They did say that the presentation stimulated reflection but called for more training as a follow-up.

In comparison, members of the second focus group (FG2) had backgrounds in diversity issues; though they expressed some anxiety, they spoke enthusiastically about the opportunity offered by the performance to practice their skills. Three additional focus groups demonstrated a mixture of the kind of responses found in the first and second. All focus group participants quoted here have been given code names to preserve anonymity.

In the meantime, we expanded our team and applied successfully for a Ford Foundation Difficult Dialogues grant. We conceptualized our Ford proposal within Bandura's self-efficacy theory (1997). When we examined our qualitative data in light of self-efficacy, we found considerable congruence. Self-efficacy theory not only helps explain the variable impact of forum theater but also suggest ways to make the performance more effective.

Bandura defines "perceived self-efficacy" as "beliefs in one's capabilities to organize and execute the courses of action required to produce given attainments" (1997, p. 3). Bandura points out that merely believing one can do something does not mean one can do it if one lacks the requisite skills. However, he refers to numerous studies showing that people who rate their self-efficacy high for a particular task will be more motivated, and will perform better, than people with more ability who rate their self-efficacy lower for that task. Bandura proposes, "Beliefs of personal efficacy constitute the key factor of human agency. If people believe they have no power to produce results, they will not attempt to make things happen" (p. 3).

**Low Self-Efficacy Versus High Self-Efficacy.**  Bandura cites several studies of teachers' "instructional efficacy" that show that low-efficacy teachers emphasize classroom control and "focus more on the subject matter than on students' development" (1997, p. 241). High-efficacy teachers are less authoritarian and more concerned with "development of their students' intrinsic interest and academic self-directedness" (p. 241). Evidence in our data matches Bandura's categorization of low- and high-efficacy instructional approaches, at least in regard to multicultural issues. For instance, members of FG1 expressed concern about classroom control. Emily argued passionately that "you should teach the subject and try to treat [the students] all the same." Beatrice agreed that her job is to teach the subject, "whether [the students] are pink or green or whatever their backgrounds are." In contrast, Clara, a higher-efficacy respondent in another group, views the teacher as a facilitator of student growth: "I think part of our job as teachers is to say, 'The reason I'm standing in front of you is because I somehow have been given grace to be able to try and make sense of your world with you, and so let me help you bring out what you're trying to say.'"

Respondents like Beatrice who expressed low self-efficacy complained about lack of diversity training: "You're just kind of thrown into the classrooms . . . , and you're not prepared or given any instructions on the differences in students." A respondent in a higher-efficacy group, Katharine, theorized that multicultural training enhanced the performance's effectiveness but that lack of such training would lessen the impact: "We've all gone through diversity training. . . . I think if we didn't have that, [the performance] might not have the same power, because we might not be able to see the things that we're meant to see."

Both lower- and higher-self-efficacy respondents perceived dealing with multicultural issues in teaching as a challenge. Higher-efficacy instructors appeared motivated to address the challenges, while lower-efficacy respondents focused on the difficulties and justifications for why they couldn't do it. For instance, instructors in FG1 know that diversity is important today but "struggle" with the dilemma of difference. They interpreted the forum theater session as advocating treating each student differently, which Emily argued would be unfair to students and would drive the teacher "crazy." Thomas considered dealing with student difference an exhausting prospect, and Beatrice thought it "just . . . not possible." Bandura observes, "The less efficacious people judge themselves to be, the more difficult the tasks will appear to them" (1997, p. 127).

**Enhancing Self-Efficacy.** Forum theater offers an opportunity for instructors to encounter two of the major determinants of self-efficacy: *mastery experience* and *vicarious experience*. By mastery experience, Bandura means that the individual practices the task and receives feedback: "spect-actors"—instructors who intervene in the sketch—gain this kind of direct experience. In his explanation of vicarious experience, Bandura refers to others "modeling" the desired behavior; forum theater audiences observe other spect-actors' interventions and see what works.

In both mastery and vicarious experience, *social comparison* comes into play: people rate their own efficacy in comparison to the success or failure of others. Bandura suggests that "seeing people similar to themselves perform successfully typically raises efficacy beliefs in observers that they themselves possess the capabilities to master comparable activities" (1997, p. 87). Seeing people fail can also raise one's sense of self-efficacy if one thinks one knows better strategies than those the model used (p. 88). However, if the observer feels that he or she lacks the ability or resources to perform well, the social comparison can lower self-efficacy beliefs: "Seeing others do well when one believes that one cannot get better is depressing, angering, and demotivating" (pp. 90–91).

We can see the dynamic of social comparison at work in audience members' responses to the professor character Ross. For FG2, a higher-efficacy group, Ross served as a "straw man," a negative model against which they could compare themselves. As Katharine put it, "We could be thinking as they're going through the scene, 'I would never do that' or 'That's really uncomfortable, and he did something wrong there.' How would [I] do it, then?" Eleanor, another participant in FG2, provoked laughter in the group by adding, "It was good for us because we could always say at least I'm better than that no matter how bad you are." Members of the higher-efficacy group said they also learned from spect-actors who demonstrated effective strategies. Katharine observed, "You learn from people who role-model correct behavior as well as incorrect behavior." FG1, a lower-efficacy group, appeared to identify with Ross, who admittedly had little diversity training. Beatrice seemed especially to empathize with Ross, arguing that he "was trying to be fair and trying to identify with the students." Since her academic discipline had not prepared her for multicultural teaching, Beatrice felt she could not measure up to spect-actors who modeled good strategies: "Sociologists and the people who have this counseling background had a very good way of handling these situations, but look, they have a background of that. If you were a mathematician, would you necessarily have that skill?" For the lower-efficacy group, the performance may actually have lowered their perceived self-efficacy because Ross, the model they saw as similar to themselves, failed, and the models who succeeded had skills they believed they lacked.

Bandura notes that personal efficacy beliefs can be enhanced by mastery and vicarious experiences. Some higher-efficacy audience members specifically referred to gains in confidence as a result of the performance. For instance, in a follow-up e-mail, Joseph (FG2) reported that prior to the performance, "I knew that I should be fair in dealing with diversity issues in the classroom, but the session gave food for more thought about *how* to be fair." He reflected on and mentally rehearsed (in what Bandura calls "cognitive rehearsal") strategies he might employ and said that the opportunity to intervene as a spect-actor "has led to a lot of confidence building already. Much of what it takes for a teacher to deal with diversity issues in classes has to do with his or her confidence. The building of that might have been the best result of the performance, especially for a new teacher like me." Another e-mail respondent said the performance "confirmed the effectiveness of my interactive teaching skills." A third noted, "I've thought about it in terms of whether I want to teach at the postsecondary level, and I came away with a new confidence and desire to do so."

In general, then, our qualitative research suggests that interactive theater may enhance the self-efficacy beliefs of higher-efficacy individuals and thus has a value for them that goes beyond "preaching to the choir." However, the performance may actually have a negative effect for lower-efficacy faculty, reducing their motivation to address diversity in the classroom and increasing their commitment to their current practice. This is ironic, given that one of the purposes of forum theater is to empower people to act (Boal, 1992).

## Conclusions

One approach to increasing the effectiveness of forum theater for lower-efficacy faculty would be to present sketches in which the challenges are not so daunting that they intimidate instructors who lack diversity skills. The strong conflicts in the scene we presented appear to elicit fear and avoidance, rather than confidence, in low-efficacy participants. Bandura observes that "dwelling on formidable aspects [weakens] people's belief in their efficacy; focusing on doable aspects [raises] their perceived efficacy" (1997, p. 57).

Another approach would be to provide multicultural training as part of a comprehensive program. We have designed our Ford "Difficult Dialogues" project, which focuses on religious dimensions of contemporary issues, to give selected faculty fellows instruction in religious literacy and conflict resolution before using forum theater as a mastery experience in which they can practice their new skills. We plan to assess fellows' perceived self-efficacy before training and after implementation of difficult dialogues in their classrooms.

## References

Bandura, A. *Self-Efficacy: The Exercise of Control.* New York: Freeman, 1997.

Boal, A. *Games for Actors and Non-Actors* (A. Jackson, trans.). London: Routledge, 1992.

Burgoyne, S. "Revising Questions and Renegotiating Consent." In P. Hutchings (ed.), *Ethics of Inquiry: Issues in the Scholarship of Teaching and Learning.* Menlo Park, Calif.: Carnegie Foundation for the Advancement of Teaching, 2002.

Freire, P. *Pedagogy of the Oppressed.* New York: Continuum, 1970.

Kaplan, M., Cook, C. E., and Steiger, J. "Using Theatre to Stage Instructional and Organizational Transformation." *Change,* 2006, *38*(3), 32–39.

Placier, P., and others. "Learning to Teach with Theatre of the Oppressed." In J. Brophy and S. Pinnegar (eds.), *Learning from Research on Teaching: Perspective, Methodology, and Representation.* Advances in Research on Teaching, no. 11. Amsterdam: Elsevier, 2005.

Schutzman, M., and Cohen-Cruz, J. (eds.). *Playing Boal: Theatre, Therapy, Activism.* New York: Routledge, 1994.

SUZANNE BURGOYNE *(Carnegie Scholar, 2000–2001) is a professor of theater at the University of Missouri-Columbia.*

PEGGY PLACIER *is an associate professor of educational leadership and policy analysis at the University of Missouri-Columbia.*

MALLORY THOMAS *is an undergraduate theater major at the University of Missouri-Columbia.*

SHARON WELCH *is a professor of religious studies at the University of Missouri-Columbia.*

CLYDE RUFFIN *is a professor of theater at the University of Missouri-Columbia.*

LISA Y. FLORES *is an assistant professor at the University of Missouri-Columbia.*

ELIF CELEBI *is a graduate student in counseling and educational psychology at the University of Missouri-Columbia.*

NOOR AZIZAN-GARDNER *is coordinator of the Chancellor's Diversity Initiative at the University of Missouri-Columbia.*

MARILYN MILLER *is interim director of the Program for Excellence in Teaching at the University of Missouri-Columbia.*

4

*The author provides a review of readings from which future faculty might explore and begin to shape a multicultural approach to teaching and learning.*

# Multicultural Teaching and Learning Resources for Preparing Future Faculty in Teaching in Higher Education Courses

*Ilene D. Alexander*

What does it mean "to teach"—both in a classroom and beyond one—as part of a career across a range of institutional types, in a particular community or group of communities, amid many student learning preferences, and within an array of cultural contexts from local to international? What happens when we teach by planning for and provoking engaged, significant learning that links to real-world experiences and questions? What can happen for learners when they talk—informally and formally—with one another and with their teachers during class time as part of a process of checking understandings, constructing analyses, and assessing the knowledge that emerges in a process of learning? What is made possible when we begin answering that initial question—What does it mean "to teach"?—via readings of pedagogical theory and personal teaching narratives by authors addressing multicultural teaching and learning within the everyday context of their theorizing and self-reflection?

These are the questions students pursue during the first six weeks of a typical Preparing Future Faculty Teaching in Higher Education course at the University of Minnesota, with an emphasis on understanding and practicing teaching for learning in a community of diverse learners. During these

NEW DIRECTIONS FOR TEACHING AND LEARNING, no. 111, Fall 2007 © Wiley Periodicals, Inc.
Published online in Wiley InterScience (www.interscience.wiley.com) • DOI: 10.1002/tl.283

first weeks, program participants experience—as we have gleaned from our observations and their evaluations—transformational learning with regard to their understanding of teaching and learning in the context of higher education in the United States. As set out by Johnson-Bailey and Alfred (2006), transformational learning involves adults in making meaning of major life events and changes through a combination of critical reflection and rational cognitive processes; additionally, in transformative learning, adults will "significantly" address "the relationship between individual, communities, and society at large" with an awareness of learning as a culturally bound experience (2006, p. 50).

As set out in the Teaching in Higher Education course design, the transformational learning process is anchored in an infusion of readings related to multicultural teaching and learning (MCT&L) in the early weeks of the semester to be accompanied by a focused week of class discussion regarding MCT&L specifically, this one coming just as students begin to develop a syllabus, assignments, teaching strategies, and assessment plans for a disciplinary or interdisciplinary course of their own design. The following annotated bibliography, therefore, first sets out common readings for that focused week. The middle section addresses diversity-related readings incorporated into earlier class sessions focused on student learning styles, active teaching and learning strategies, and "backward" course design. In closing, I review what we have learned about this approach, based on an analysis of student survey responses.

## Framing a Multicultural Approach to Teaching and Learning

### Core Readings

Of the following four core readings, two specifically explore MCT&L in science disciplines, two are written by senior scholars, and two link active learning and teaching strategies to MCT&L in order to address student-student as well as student-teacher interactions as important components of multicultural course design. Because a majority of our students expect to teach in science classrooms and have few opportunities to observe active or multicultural learning (especially in large classrooms) on our campus, they remain skeptical at midsemester about the applicability of MCT&L to their course design and overall teaching philosophy. At the same time, students from humanities, social sciences, education, and professional disciplines are eager to move beyond classroom assessment techniques and variations on class discussion strategies as MCT&L tools. The following readings bring a specificity that allows each broad grouping of students to analyze possibilities and adapt practices.

Nelson, C. E. "Student Diversity Requires Different Approaches to College Teaching, Even in Math and Science." *American Behavioral Scientist,* 1996, *40*(2), 165–175.

Between the opening line—"When I first encountered them, the arguments challenging professors to address diversity in our classrooms seemed . . . not likely to have any positive effect in most science courses, certainly not those I taught in biology"—and a closing paragraph advocating "a switch from seeing our roles as sorting out the unfit to . . . striving to maximize the success of all students in mastering our disciplines," Nelson sets out specific examples of teachers taking first steps to incorporate active learning into everyday teaching, with the effect of increasing equity and achievement for students across diverse backgrounds.

Kolodny, A. "Teaching and Learning in a World of Cognitive Diversity." *Failing the Future: A Dean Looks at Higher Education in the 21st Century.* Raleigh, N.C.: Duke University Press, 1998.

Building on generalizations about culturally inflected learning styles, Kolodny illuminates ways in which teachers in research-extensive institutions have built cognitively robust learning objects, student learning strategies, classroom teaching practices, and disciplinary expectations for excellence as part of "[thinking] about not only *what* [faculty] will be teaching but *who* they will be teaching and *how*" (p. 169). It is this junction of what, who, and how that future faculty need to investigate as they shape MCT&L practices and become "prepared to teach everyone well" (p. 172).

Miller, A. T. "The Multicultural Lab: Diversity Issues in STEM Classes." In M. L. Ouellett (ed.), *Teaching Inclusively: Resources for Course, Department, and Institutional Change in Higher Education.* Stillwater, Okla.: New Forums, 2006.

Most future faculty enrolled in Teaching in Higher Education are already teaching—or will soon begin teaching—in lab, discussion, or recitation sections attached to large courses enrolling 150 to 500 students. What can we do about retention and to encourage achievement in our sections, they ask, if the large class models passive learning or, worse still, operates to "weed out weak learners"? The reasons I return again and again to Miller's selection is revealed in the active reading assignments students compose in response to this core reading. The segments addressing Miller's chapter typically reflect understanding along two common threads: (1) the need to use active learning to break students out of familiar, monocultural groupings by using random or more formalized pairings and small groups throughout a course, and (2) the need to move away from "gatekeeping" by, for example, balancing inductive and deductive approaches, moving away from culturally bound assumptions when interacting with students, and drawing problems from a range of real-world institutional and social contexts.

*Teaching Inclusively,* the anthology edited by Ouellett that includes Miller's chapter, offers numerous resources that future faculty can draw on as they become involved in shaping departmental or university policy or advocating for and creating faculty development programming.

Center for Teaching and Learning. *Teaching for Inclusion: Diversity in the College Classroom.* Chapel Hill: University of North Carolina, 1997. http://ctl.unc.edu/TeachforInclusion.pdf. Accessed June 28, 2006.

Prenger, S. M. (ed.). *Teaching for Inclusion: A Resource Book for Nebraska University Faculty.* Lincoln: University of Nebraska, Teaching and Learning Center, 1999.

The North Carolina and Nebraska texts are the only core readings that specifically provide analysis along identity axes. Students can be individually assigned to read and prepare a comparative synthesis of parallel sections in each book. Coming together (for example, using a constructive controversy or jigsaw of multiple readings) helps students deepen their practice of speaking honestly with peers and become aware of resources they can consult across a lifelong collaborative learning process regarding MCT&L. Although the contexts differ (UNC's southern urban setting versus Nebraska's midwestern and more rural context), both texts draws on student voices and point to appropriate teaching strategies, with the Nebraska text offering full, easy-to-use sample teaching documents.

## Infused Readings on Student Learning, Course Design, and Teacher Philosophy

Tatum, B. D. "Talking About Race, Learning About Racism: Application of Racial Identity Development Theory in the College Classroom." *Harvard Educational Review,* 1992, 62(1), 1–24.

Early in the semester, I ask students to read and discuss racial identity development alongside a fairly common set of resources on student learning. For students already teaching or hoping soon to teach courses dealing with cultural diversity and social issues, it is additionally important to understand that undergraduates vary with regard to development along a racial identity continuum and that this variation operates alongside learning styles in shaping student resistance to and engagement with learning. By reading Tatum's discussion of common points of conflict and reasons for conflict, students consider what they might do to plan class sessions and select learning strategies that will help students understand these fundamental but also shifting and sometime convergent points of development.

Saunders, S., and Kardia, D. "Creating Inclusive College Classrooms." In *A Guidebook for University of Michigan Graduate Student Instructors.* Ann Arbor: University of Michigan, 2004. http://www.crlt.umich.edu/multiteaching/multipapers.html. Accessed May 30, 2007.

Center for Research on Learning and Teaching. "The Effect of Student Diversity on Student Learning at the University of Michigan: Faculty and GSI Perspectives." CRLT Occasional Paper no. 12. Ann Arbor: University of Michigan, 1999. http://www.crlt.umich.edu/multiteaching/multipapers.html. Accessed May 30, 2007.

Chesler, M. A. "Perceptions of Faculty Behavior by Students of Color." CRLT Occasional Paper no. 7. Ann Arbor: University of Michigan, 1997. http://www.crlt.umich.edu/multiteaching/multipapers.html. Accessed May 30, 2007.

"Broadly speaking," Saunders and Kardia state, "the inclusiveness of a classroom will depend upon the kinds of interactions that occur between and among you and the students in the classroom." The factors they name—and then thoroughly substantiate by unraveling common assumptions in a style of do and don't suggestions—include course content, instructor assumptions and awareness, pedagogical strategies, diversity of students' backgrounds, and teaching philosophy as it shapes communication and decisions about teaching and learning. Students report that incorporation of this article into readings focused on course and syllabus design opens them up to thinking about diversity as integral rather than supplemental or for someone else to teach and address.

Two other readings from the Web site of the University of Michigan's Center for Research on Learning and Teaching are excellent companion pieces to common future faculty readings focused on objectives-driven and backward course design. The short narratives in "The Effect of Student Diversity on Student Learning" describe how teaching assistants and faculty across nine disciplines consciously develop inclusive curricula and classroom climates. To understand the importance of inclusive teaching for student retention and success, I ask participants to read "Perceptions of Faculty Behavior by Students of Color" and to discuss how student comments challenge or support their assumptions about the role of MCT&L in higher education.

Horton, M. "Islands of Decency" and "Workshops." In M. Horton, *The Long Haul: An Autobiography of Myles Horton.* New York: Anchor/Doubleday, 1990.
hooks, b. "Embracing Change: Teaching in a Multicultural World" and "Paulo Freire." In b. hooks, *Teaching to Transgress: Education as the Practice of Freedom.* New York: Routledge, 1994.

Anthologies and readers focusing on these broad theoretical formulations—adaptations of work by the Brazilian educator Paulo Freire—are plentiful and rich. But in a one-semester course, students seem unable to handle this additional layer of deeply theoretical reading. By introducing personal voices at the same time that students complete a first revision of teaching philosophy statements, it is possible to "examine critically the way we as teachers conceptualize what the space for learning should be like" (hooks, 1994, p. 39). Through an interactive lecture, reading of the recommended chapters, and participation in a learning circle discussion (Horton, 1990, pp. 144–160), students are able to think about ways they might "build a program [teaching practice] that will deal with things as they are now and as they ought to be at the same time," which Horton called a two-eyed approach to education (p. 131).

## Conclusion

Johnson-Bailey and Alfred (2006) speak of transformational MCT&L as involving a "troubling" of assigned readings with and for students—"always guiding them to examine their assumptions and the author's perspective and to query whose interests are being served." By assigning the writing of journal entries, active reading assignments, or reaction or difficulty papers, we give "students space to think critically and reflect on ideas" at micro, mezzo, and macro levels (p. 56). The core and infused readings serve, then, as starting points for that process of troubling.

As part of a programmatic review and revitalization of the Teaching in Higher Education course in 2004 and 2005, I analyzed previous end-of-term open-ended evaluations and surveys of students' pre- and postcourse confidence levels surrounding MCT&L. I noticed two things regarding MCT&L: in noting what could be dropped from the course, a number of students had written comments about diversity and MCT&L discussions; also, the precourse/postcourse gains score tended to be quite small for the item related to confidence in addressing and supporting MCT&L. My two assignments in the course revitalization were, first, to consider changes we might make in core readings and homework assignments and what resources we made available to students who opted to develop their fifty- to seventy-five-minute joint facilitation session during the focused MCT&L class session and, second, to complete a preliminary assessment at the end of the 2005–06 academic year.

In meeting the first charge, four guiding principles emerged—and inform the choices I outline here: (1) authors of core readings should be senior scholars from at least two broad disciplinary groups who write to illuminate their own thinking about MCT&L issues with regard to teaching, learning, and university policy; (2) assigned readings should link active learning strategies to MCT&L as an everyday teaching endeavor; (3) Web resources should point to materials that help future faculty think about students' perspectives and cultural contexts; and (4) an active reading assignment should call on students to reflect on ways of incorporating MCT&L awareness and strategies into their own teaching practices.

To meet the second charge and begin assessing the impact of this particular revitalization, I collected and analyzed confidence data within pre- and postcourse confidence surveys, which we had not changed during the course revitalization. These surveys include an item asking students to respond by indicating (on a 1–7 scale ranging from "not at all" to "completely" confident) to the question "How confident do you feel in your ability to support and address student diversity?" The findings from four courses I recently cotaught are reported in Table 4.1.

Across these four sections, we are able to see a positive trend in the gains score and, in the standard deviation, a tendency for confidence scores to cluster together rather than split toward either the high or the low end of the confidence spectrum. Furthermore, the strongest gains are linked to the two classes where the coteachers and a student cofacilitation team each took responsibility for session presentations, activities, discussions, and assessments. To consider long-term impact and to consider course changes we might make for future years, we will analyze active reading homework as well as a selection of students' course portfolios and will interview a rep-

**Table 4.1. MCT&L Confidence Scores**

| Section | Number of Students | Mean (Precourse/ Postcourse) | Standard Deviation (Precourse/ Postcourse) | Gains Score | Cofacilitation |
|---|---|---|---|---|---|
| Spring 2005 | 21 | 4.0/5.63 | 1.58/0.90 | 1.63 | Yes, by teachers and students |
| Spring 2005 | 12 | 4.67/5.5 | 0.72/1.00 | 0.83 | No, and only one teacher present |
| Spring 2006 | 24 | 4.0/6.0 | 1.01/0.73 | 2.00 | Yes, by teachers and students |
| Summer 2006 | 13 | 5.3/5.9 | 1.48/0.95 | 0.60 | No, and only one teacher present |

resentative group of students who have gone on to teach courses of their own design. I expect that hearing from students will continue to "trouble" and invigorate our ways of infusing and focusing on multicultural teaching and learning in Teaching in Higher Education.

## Reference

Johnson Bailey, J., and Alfred, M. V. "Transformational Teaching and the Practices of Black Women Adult Educators." *New Directions for Adult and Continuing Education*, no. 109. San Francisco: Jossey-Bass, 2006.

*ILENE D. (IDA) ALEXANDER coordinates the Preparing Future Faculty and Multicultural Teaching and Learning fellowship grant programs at the Center for Teaching and Learning at the University of Minnesota–Twin Cities.*

NEW DIRECTIONS FOR TEACHING AND LEARNING • DOI: 10.1002/tl

5

*The authors describe and evaluate an approach to engaging students in exploring social identities, understanding inequality, and identifying avenues for individual and collective action for greater social justice.*

# Intergroup Dialogue: A Critical-Dialogic Approach to Learning About Difference, Inequality, and Social Justice

*Biren (Ratnesh) A. Nagda, Patricia Gurin*

Intergroup dialogue (IGD) is an educational endeavor that brings together students from two or more social identity groups to build relationships across cultural and power differences, to raise consciousness of inequalities, to explore the similarities and differences in experiences across identity groups, and to strengthen individual and collective capacities to promote social justice. IGDs, comprised of about twelve to sixteen students, meet weekly over a period of ten to fourteen weeks. Trained peer facilitators use an educational curriculum that integrates multiple dimensions of learning: content and process learning; intellectual and affective engagement; individual reflection and group dialogue; individual, intergroup, and institutional analyses; affinity-based and heterogeneous groupings; and individual and collective action. Readings, reflective writing, and a collaborative action project complement the in-class dialogues (see Zúñiga, Nagda, Chesler, and Cytron-Walker, 2007, for a detailed description).

Intergroup dialogue builds on the traditions of diversity and social justice education but offers an innovative alternative. Diversity education aims to promote feelings of unity, tolerance, and acceptance *within the existing societal structure* (Sleeter and Grant, 2003). Social justice education teaches

NEW DIRECTIONS FOR TEACHING AND LEARNING, no. 111, Fall 2007 © Wiley Periodicals, Inc.
Published online in Wiley InterScience (www.interscience.wiley.com) • DOI: 10.1002/tl.284

students about group-based inequalities, aims to promote greater social structural equality, and prepares students for citizenship in culturally pluralistic societies. However, what is generally missing from these two approaches is an explicit focus on cross-group interactions in the classroom as a crucial nexus of learning. Intergroup dialogue addresses this missing focus on classroom interaction, stressing three components of a critical-dialogic approach:

- Critical analysis and understanding of difference and dominance
- Discursive engagement across differences
- Sustained and conjoint community building and conflict engagement

## Critical Analysis and Understanding of Difference and Dominance

Critical analysis, in IGD, refers to understanding inequalities as contextualized in structural systems rather than just in individual differences (Miller, 1994; Nagda, 2006). Intergroup dialogue situates group differences and inequalities in the context of sociostructural and power relations, such as institutional racism or patriarchy. Critical consciousness cannot be imposed on the students, nor is it immediate; it is both developmental and cyclical in nature. In the early sessions, students reflect on multiple social group memberships—including identities of race, ethnicity, gender, class, sexual orientation, national origin, religion and spirituality, ability, and age. They dialogue about the identities that are important to them. They also reflect and discuss identities that they do not consider important and inquire why that is. Students reflect later on their socialization into identities and examine the influence of peers and family, cultural sources, and social institutions (Harro, 2000). Thus IGDs help students personalize the connection between identities and inequalities. Students continue their conscientization (Freire, 1970) through inquiry on the interconnections among educational, occupational, legal, and other institutions in structuring systems of unequal power and privilege.

IGD research shows strong evidence for students' increased critical consciousness. In two studies using pretest-posttest surveys, students report thinking more about their social group memberships (Nagda and Zúñiga, 2003) and thinking more complexly about larger societal and historical influences on their own and others' behaviors (Nagda, Gurin, and Lopez, 2003). Particularly noteworthy are two studies focusing on students' causal understanding of inequalities. For example, one study of first-year undergraduates comparing IGD participants to a matched comparison group of nonparticipants (matched on race, gender, residency in or out of state, and residence hall) found that participants thought more structurally about racial and ethnic inequalities than their counterparts did (Lopez, Gurin, and Nagda, 1998) at the end of the course. Participants more strongly agreed with such statements as "In the United States, there are still great differences between social levels—what one can achieve in life depends mainly on one's

NEW DIRECTIONS FOR TEACHING AND LEARNING • DOI: 10.1002/tl

family background" and less strongly agreed with such statements as "A person's racial background in this society does not interfere with achieving everything he or she wants to achieve." The study also checked for self-selection into the course but did not find differences at entry into college.

## Discursive Engagement Across Differences

Discursive engagement refers to the nature of communicative interactions students have with each other. Table 5.1 differentiates three communication modes—debate, discussion, and dialogue. *Debates* in the classroom are used for students to use evidence-based thinking on issues, develop verbal presentation skills, and strengthen abilities to influence others by defending one's position and countering differing positions (Keller, Whitaker, and Burke, 2001). *Discussion* may be used for deliberative decision making (Parker, 2003) or be more conversational to foster self-awareness and self-critique and may consist of affiliating with others through an appreciation of diversity of perspectives (Brookfield and Preskill, 2005). The concepts of debate and discussion are generally understood, but dialogue has a particular meaning in this context that requires further explanation.

Dialogue aims to foster empathic connection, understanding through inquiry, and mutual respect (Nagda and others, 1999). Dialogue practitioners agree that it is an open-ended process that allows all participants to gain new or deeper ways of thinking, to build relationships with others, and to work effectively on collaborative projects. Linda Teurfs, in an interview with Weiler (1994), identified four building blocks crucial to dialogue: suspending judgment, deep listening, identifying assumptions, and reflection and inquiry. Engagement encompasses the verbal and nonverbal, the intellectual and affective, and the individual and group levels. Careful facilitation in dialogue includes all students, helps them build connections among perspectives by identifying differences and similarities, and presses for both personalization and deeper understanding of assumptions that underlie perspectives (Bohm, 1990; Flick, 1998; Yankelovich, 1999).

IGD may at times use all three modes, although dialogue predominates over debate and discussion. Given the emphasis on critical analysis of inequality in IGD, dialogue serves as a liberatory communicative process that is both pedagogical and political, building relationships among people who are differentially affected by social stratification and asymmetric power relations. Interrelated learning activities, such as social identity affinity groups (Zúñiga and Nagda, 1993) and fishbowls (Schoem, Zúñiga, and Nagda, 1993), help explain how differential privilege and power affect individuals in the separate groups and across the groups in dialogue. Instead of differences being divisive, explicit acknowledgment and dialogue about the differentials can facilitate more connective relationships (Collins, 1996).

Two studies speak directly to the purposefulness of dialogic engagement processes. First, Yeakley's qualitative study of change processes in

**Table 5.1. Approaches to Discursive Engagement**

| | Debate | Discussion | Intergroup Dialogue |
|---|---|---|---|
| Understanding Difference and Dominance | | *• Differences as diversity—differences are seen as individual differences, the result of individual prejudices and stereotypes.* *• Differences in context of sociocultural and power relations—differences are seen to represent or emerge from cultural differences and unequal power (dominant-subordinated) relationships; analyses of structural and institutional systems of oppression and privilege; consideration of differential social identity development processes for participants* | |
| Goals of Discursive Engagement | • To clarify pros and cons of issues<br>• To develop critical thinking skills | • To generate different perspectives on issues<br>• To increase perspective taking and critical thinking skills<br>• To weigh or make decisions among different options | • To increase critical self-awareness and social awareness<br>• To increase intergroup communication, understanding, and collaborative actions |
| Modes of Discursive Engagement | • A back-and-forth of arguments<br>• Perseverance and advocacy of perspective<br>• One right answer, determined by force of argument, identifying flaws in others' logic | • Openness to different perspectives<br>• Disparate or connected knowing<br>• Varies in personalization and contextualization<br>• Cognitive inquiry | • Emphasis on connected knowing (discerning similarities and differences)<br>• Personalization, affective expression, and empathic relations<br>• Contextualization in larger social systems<br>• Self-inquiry and other-inquiry |
| Role of Community and Conflict | • Community not considered<br>• Fight to convince other<br>• Defined by positions | • Community as group of individuals, with emphasis on similarities<br>• Recognition of conflict of ideas without critical exploration<br>• Diffusion and compromise ("we can agree to disagree") | • Diverse community, acknowledges differences as well as similarities<br>• Conflicts are surfaced and normalized; treated as opportunities for learning<br>• Search for collaborative possibilities and social justice |

intergroup contact (1998) found that sharing and hearing personal experiences in a supportive climate differentiated positive and negative intergroup contact experiences. When personal experiences revolved around similarities, participants developed cross-group friendships. However, if personal experiences brought up differences, participants gained an understanding of multiple perspectives. If the differences were further understood vis-à-vis social identities, participants gained greater intergroup understanding. Second, Nagda's quantitative study (2006) asked students to indicate the extent to which a set of communication processes had contributed to their learning at the end of intergroup dialogues. Factor analysis revealed four distinct processes. Two processes reflect dialogic engagement: appreciating difference (learning about others and hearing about different points of view) and engaging self (complementing learning about others with sharing of one's own perspectives and rethinking them). Two others reflect critical engagement: critical self-reflection (examination of one's ideas, experiences, and perspectives in the context of inequality, privilege, and oppression) and alliance building (relating to and thinking about collaborating with others in taking actions toward social justice). Together these studies show that the deeper the personalization and the greater the contextualization of issues in intergroup dialogue, the wider the range of learning for students, from intergroup friendships to intergroup understanding and collaborative actions.

## Sustained and Conjoint Community Building and Conflict Engagement

Some critics may argue that IGD is "just talk" and that talking about identity, difference, and inequality only escalates conflict and separation among groups. Our research and practice say otherwise. The communicative possibility embedded in intergroup dialogue provides an understanding of societal divisions and inequalities but also demonstrates that we are neither confined nor destined to remain static in social estrangement. It does mean, though, that we have to actively and earnestly reach across our differences and, as Collins (1996) says, "work toward replacing judgments by category with new ways of thinking and acting. Refusing to do so stifles effective coalition and social change" (p. 223). It also means that we must grapple honestly with the place and role of conflict and community as we engage deeply with and across our differences.

In IGD, community is built across differences and through the deep exploration of differences and conflicts. In contrast to debate, in which community is not of concern, and to discussion, where community is built around superordinate groups (such as "all students"), community in intergroup dialogue honors separate social group identities and encourages an appreciation of a common group identity constructed around alliance building and the work of social justice. Whereas conflicts in debates are around positions and in discussion around ideas, conflicts in intergroup dialogues are connected to identities, social structures, and relationships. Conflict engagement thus plays an important role in deepening the dialogic relating, expanding students' understanding of the issues that influence conflicts, and building students' capacity to work through disagreements and conflicts in productive ways. When conflicts emerge in the group, they are not taken as a sign of failed dialogue; rather, they are opportunities for deeper learning. Similarly, working through conflicts is not automatically assumed to lead to a breach in the relationship; in fact, it is exactly because of working through conflicts that a deeper sense of community is developed.

How do we sustain engagement with differences in ways that connect us and not estrange us further? Community building and conflict engagement are processes that unfold and develop over the duration of the dialogues. We take an intentional approach to preparing and building the container for dialogue, engaging conflict (that is, surfacing and responding to conflict), and applying the learning. In the first one or two sessions in IGD, explicit attention is given to forming engagement guidelines and building a learning community. Facilitators emphasize that talking about the issues of difference, identity, and inequality is not easy and that disagreements and conflicts are part and parcel of good dialogues.

As the intergroup dialogues progress, we use a variety of approaches to surface and respond to conflicts. In the case of overt disagreements and conflicts, facilitators usually name the conflicts instead of avoiding them. They emphasize dialogic engagement by modeling and facilitating active listening, perspective taking, and asking questions so that the different perspectives are clearly understood. With more subtle or covert conflicts, facilitators pay particular attention to the dynamics of privilege and oppression that may emerge in the group, such as dominating talking time by a few members, unequal emotional sharing, privileging objective information over emotions, denying other people's experiences of discrimination or marginalization, and one-way questioning by dominant group members of subordinated group members (Narayan, 1988). When this happens, facilitators may "freeze frame" and ask students to reflect on and voice how they were feeling and what they were noticing in that particular moment. To continue unpacking the disagreements and conflicts in any instance, facilitators guide the group in mapping the emergent perspectives and probing *who,* from *which* identities, is saying *what* and the consequent impact on dialogue participants. They further contextualize the emerging differences and similarities in the dynamics of dominance and explore ways to bridge across the differences. Another reflective structure that facilitators use is the "dialogue about the dialogue" to explore students' experiences of the IGD to date, both positive and negative, and to think of ways to deepen the dialogue (Zúñiga, Nagda, Chesler, and Cytron-Walker, 2007).

Just as community building prepares for deeper conflict engagement, conflict engagement has consequences for strengthening the community.

Opportunities for students to jointly apply their learning through collaborative projects are an important component of IGDs. For the Intergroup Collaboration Project, teams of three or four students work together on an action project supporting diversity and justice on the campus or in the community—brainstorming ideas, selecting an action, and planning, implementing, and debriefing their learning. Students report several lessons from these intergroup collaborations: a deeper understanding of inequality; an acute awareness of how issues of dominance, privilege, and oppression get enacted in their own teams; and a heightened confidence in using their learning to educate and inform others, challenge oppressive remarks and actions, and build alliances for social justice.

The practice and research of intergroup dialogue also reveal that community building and conflict engagement are useful for purposeful actions and commitments outside the group. Gurin, Peng, Lopez, and Nagda (1999), in their study comparing first-year students in an intergroup relations course to a matched comparison group of nonparticipants, found that students of color in the course perceived less divisiveness on campus than nonparticipants; they less strongly agreed that thinking about groups was largely divisive or that the university's emphasis on diversity meant that they could not talk honestly about racial, ethnic, and gender issues. There was no difference for white students and nonparticipants. In terms of commonality, they found that the course had differential effects across race. The course had a main effect for white students' feelings of commonality of interests and values with students of color. For students of color, commonality in values with white students increased for those who were more strongly identified racially or ethnically. However, the course had a main positive effect for the quality of interactions that students of color had with white students. The course also had a positive impact on all students' positive beliefs about conflict. Gurin, Nagda, and Lopez (2004) surveyed the same students four years later and found that course participants were more interested in politics, participated more in campus politics, and more highly anticipated helping their groups or community and promoting racial and ethnic understanding than the matched control students did.

A series of studies using pretest-posttest surveys of participants have further investigated the influence of classroom teaching and learning methods on community and conflict outcomes. First, Nagda and Zúñiga (2003) found that students' value for the dialogic engagement was positively related to their affirmative views about conflict (for example, "I believe that conflicts and disagreements in the classroom enrich the learning process" and "I think that conflicts between social identity groups can help clarify misunderstandings that each group has about the other"). Positive influences were also seen for one measure of community—bridging differences (for example, "I want to bridge differences between different social identity groups"). Second, Gurin, Nagda, and Lopez (2004) showed that the informational content and intergroup interactions in intergroup dialogue help build a learning community that allows for learning about one's own group and other groups, reflecting more on one's own group, and bridging differences between groups. The motivation to bridge differences was directly related to greater confidence in reducing one's own prejudiced thoughts and behaviors and promoting diversity with and among others. Zúñiga's research (2004) found that students defined actions similar to what they were doing in the dialogues—taking risks, talking with others, and educating themselves and others. One could make a case for intergroup dialogues becoming an in vivo learning environment where students experiment with and refine their motivation and skills for action outside the dialogues. In a later study, Nagda (2006) found that the four communication processes mentioned earlier—appreciating difference, engaging self, critical self-reflection, and alliance building—have a concerted impact on bridging differences. Most interestingly, the communication process of alliance building—working through differences and conflicts, challenging biases and assumptions, and developing commitments to social justice—deepens the desire to bridge differences.

## Advancing the Scholarship of Teaching and Learning of Intergroup Dialogues

To build on the strengths of the existing research and address its limitations, the scholarship of intergroup dialogues is now extended in a multiuniversity research study. Nine universities (seven public, two private) are collaborating on this project: Arizona State University; Occidental College; Syracuse University; University of California, San Diego; University of Maryland, College Park; University of Massachusetts at Amherst; University of Michigan, Ann Arbor; University of Texas at Austin; and University of Washington, Seattle. The research project is theoretically driven; it involves both race and gender dialogues in which we aim to have an equal number of white men, white women, men of color, and women of color participate; and it uses random assignment of interested students to an intergroup dialogue or a wait-list control group. We elaborate on the main components of the project and how they address the limitations of the existing research as follows.

*Theoretically driven study.* Unlike previous studies, the multiuniversity project specifically tests a theory of intergroup dialogue that links the IGD intervention to outcomes via individual psychological and situational communication processes. The project also extends the range of outcomes considered—intergroup understanding of inequalities, intergroup communication, and intergroup collaboration—and the breadth of processes examined—individual, situational, and group-level.

*Addressing internal validity.* Because of the lack of studies using matched comparison groups of students, attribution of outcomes solely to intergroup dialogue are difficult to assess. The multiuniversity study uses randomized assignment of students to the experimental group (the intergroup dialogue) and to a wait-list control group from applicants interested in participating in either a race or a gender dialogue. The randomized assignment, combined with the theoretical model, will help clarify not only if intergroup dialogue are effective or not but also what mechanisms increase or reduce effectiveness.

*Addressing external validity.* Because previous studies have been conducted exclusively at single institutions, the findings cannot necessarily be generalized. The multiuniversity project addresses the limitation of generalizability through its collaboration of ten colleges and universities across the United States.

*Generalization across participants.* The current study balances participants by both race and gender: ideally, there are four women of color, four white women, four men of color, and four white men in each race and gender dialogue. The study will thus for the first time enable us to look at similarities and differences across these demographic groups.

*Mixed-methods research.* The multiuniversity study uses both quantitative and qualitative methods. On the quantitative side, we use a pretest-posttest survey as well as a follow-up survey one year after participation. Qualitatively, in-class reflection papers will capture the emotional processes evoked by experiential activities, final papers will be analyzed for both processes (such as engaging self and critical self-reflection) and outcomes (such as empathy and structural understanding of inequality), and individual interviews and videotaping of select sessions will help elucidate descriptive information about learning outcomes as well as individual and group processes.

## Conclusion

The scholarship of teaching and learning of intergroup dialogues shows that involving students in intellectual and affective interactions with fellow classmates—voicing their convictions and trepidations, listening to each other's desires for connection and fears of betrayal, inquiring into how each of their experiences is influenced by the larger social realities, and knowing deeply that one's own sense of humanity is interconnected to how we are with each other—can contribute to democratic living just not politically but personally as well. The multiuniversity intergroup dialogue research project will deepen and expand our understanding of the unique critical-dialogical engagement as one avenue to empower students to know and to learn, to care and to act, and to be and to interact in more socially just ways in the world.

## References

Bohm, D. *On Dialogue.* Ojai, Calif.: David Bohm Seminars, 1990.

Brookfield, S., and Preskill, S. *Discussion as a Way of Teaching: Tools and Techniques for Democratic Classrooms.* San Francisco: Jossey-Bass, 2005.

Collins, P. H. "Toward a New Vision: Race, Class, and Gender as Categories of Analysis and Connection." In K. Rosenblum and T. Travis (eds.), *The Meaning of Difference: American Constructions of Race, Sex and Gender, Social Class, and Sexual Orientation.* New York: McGraw-Hill, 1996.

Flick, D. *From Debate to Dialogue: Using the Understanding Process to Transform Our Conversations.* Boulder, Colo.: Orchid, 1998.

Freire, P. *Pedagogy of the Oppressed.* New York: Continuum, 1970.

Gurin, P., Nagda, B. A., and Lopez, G. E. "The Benefits of Diversity in Education for Democratic Citizenship." *Journal of Social Issues,* 2004, *60*(1), 17–34.

Gurin, P., Peng, T., Lopez, G. E., and Nagda, B. A. "Context, Identity, and Intergroup Relations." In D. Prentice and D. Miller (eds.), *Cultural Divides: Understanding and Overcoming Group Conflict.* New York: Russell Sage Foundation, 1999.

Harro, B. "The Cycle of Socialization." In M. Adams, L. A. Bell, and P. Griffin (eds.), *Readings for Diversity and Social Justice: An Anthology on Racism, Anti-Semitism, Sexism, Heterosexism, Ableism, and Classism.* New York: Routledge, 2000.

Keller, T. E., Whittaker, J. K., and Burke, T. K. "Student Debates in Policy Courses: Promoting Policy Practice Skills and Knowledge Through Active Learning." *Journal of Social Work Education,* 2001, *37*(2), 343–355.

Lopez, G. E., Gurin, P., and Nagda, B. A. "Education and Understanding Structural Causes for Group Inequalities." *Journal of Political Psychology,* 1998, *19*(2), 305–329.

Miller, F. "Why We Chose to Address Oppression." In E. Y. Cross, J. H. Katz, F. A. Miller, and E. W. Seashore (eds.), *The Promise of Diversity: Over 40 Voices Discuss Strategies for Eliminating Discrimination in Organizations.* Burr Ridge, Ill.: Irwin, 1994.

Nagda, B. A. "Breaking Barriers, Crossing Boundaries, Building Bridges: Communication Processes in Intergroup Dialogues." *Journal of Social Issues,* 2006, *62*(3), 553–576.

Nagda, B. A., Gurin, P., and Lopez, G. E. "Transformative Pedagogy for Democracy and Social Justice." *Race, Ethnicity and Education,* 2003, *6*(2), 165–191.

Nagda, B. A., and others. "Intergroup Dialogues: An Innovative Approach to Teaching About Diversity and Justice in Social Work Programs." *Journal of Social Work Education,* 1999, *35*(3), 433–449.

Nagda, B. A., and Zúñiga, X. "Fostering Meaningful Racial Engagement Through Intergroup Dialogues." *Group Processes and Intergroup Relations,* 2003, *6*(1), 111–128.

Narayan, U. "Working Together Across Difference: Some Considerations on Emotions and Political Practice." *Hypatia,* 1988, *3*(2), 31–47.

Parker, W. *Teaching Democracy: Unity and Diversity in Public Life.* New York: Teachers College Press, 2003.

Schoem, D., Zúñiga, X., and Nagda, B. A. "Exploring One's Background: The Fishbowl Exercise." In D. Schoem, L. Frankel, X. Zúñiga, and E. Lewis (eds.), *Multicultural Teaching in the University.* Westport, Conn.: Praeger, 1993.

Sleeter, C. E., and Grant, C. *Making Choices for Multicultural Education: Five Approaches to Race, Class, and Gender.* Hoboken, N.J.: Wiley, 2003.

Weiler, J. "Finding a Shared Meaning: Reflections on Dialogue. An Interview with Linda Teurfs." *Seeds,* 1994, *11*(1), 5–10.

Yankelovich, D. *The Magic of Dialogue: Transforming Conflict into Cooperation.* New York: Simon & Schuster, 1999.

Yeakley, A. "The Nature of Prejudice Change: Positive and Negative Change Processes Arising from Intergroup Contact Experiences." Unpublished doctoral dissertation, University of Michigan, 1998.

Zúñiga, X. "The Ripple Effects of Talking About Race and Gender: Moving from Dialogue to Action." Paper presented at the American Educational Research Association (AERA) National Conference, San Diego, Calif., April 2004.

Zúñiga, X., and Nagda, B. A. "Identity Group Exercise." In D. Schoem, L. Frankel, X. Zúñiga, and E. Lewis (eds.), *Multicultural Teaching in the University.* Westport, Conn.: Praeger, 1993.

Zúñiga, X., Nagda, B. A., Chesler, M., and Cytron-Walker, A. *Intergroup Dialogues in Higher Education: Meaningful Learning About Social Justice.* ASHE Higher Education Report Series, no. 32, iss. 4. Hoboken, NJ: Wiley, 2007.

*BIREN (RATNESH) A. NAGDA is associate professor of social work and director of the Intergroup Dialogue, Education and Action (IDEA) Center at the University of Washington.*

*PATRICIA GURIN is the Nancy Cantor Distinguished Professor, Emerita, of psychology and women's studies, and the director of research for the Program on Intergroup Relations at the University of Michigan.*

6

*This chapter explores the challenges of assessing multi-cultural learning in a service-learning course and offers a variety of strategies for measuring student development.*

# Acts of Diversity: Assessing the Impact of Service-Learning

*Jo B. Paoletti, Eden Segal, Christina Totino*

AMST 498J is a humanities service-learning course in American studies that brings university students—most of them comfortable-to-affluent Caucasians—to a Boys and Girls Club to interact with high school students—most of them poverty-level or modestly middle-class blacks and Latinos. Approximately forty students sign up for this course each semester, most looking for an upper-level course outside their major to fulfill university requirements. They engage in service-learning in subsections of eight to twelve students, each with one or two undergraduate teaching assistants who supervise them at the service site. Our course description and learning objectives pertain to the intersection of individual human experience, social issues, and critical thinking. Excavating and examining attitudes and beliefs about diversity is an essential subtext of the course.

For assessing learning about diversity in this particular class, we believe that qualitative, interpretive methods (Gelmon and others, 2001) are most appropriate. In part this is due to our educational training, but it also flows from our conviction that scholarship of teaching methods should be aligned with methods commonly used in nonpedagogical research in the same field. In the case of American studies, that would include close, self-reflexive analysis of texts, the method primarily used in this study. Students in the course produce a variety of written materials and are engaged in weekly service, which can be observed and evaluated. We sought ways to use student

NEW DIRECTIONS FOR TEACHING AND LEARNING, no. 111, Fall 2007 © Wiley Periodicals, Inc.
Published online in Wiley InterScience (www.interscience.wiley.com) • DOI: 10.1002/tl.285

47

writing and on-site performance in both ongoing formative assessment and in the final summative assessment for grading purposes.

The two interrelated challenges we have encountered are establishing where students are at the beginning of the service-learning experience and identifying advancement from those initial positions, particularly as related to multicultural learning. Over time we realized that effective assessment— whether formative or summative—required students to be involved in the assessment process. It became essential to the course for students to develop the ability to describe their own starting point honestly and accurately, to monitor and assess learning as it occurs, and to be able to articulate—again, honestly and accurately—their own position at the conclusion of the course. Ultimately, we turned to the students in the class to help us solve these riddles: In classes dealing with cultural diversity, how can we tell what, how, and when someone is learning? How do we fairly assess and grade student performance when it may well be just that, a performance, intended to please the teacher but not necessarily representing the student's actual learning?

## Looking for Evidence of Learning

We require students to demonstrate learning in several ways. The modes of the interpretive evidence are presented here from the simple (minute papers) to the more complex (final portfolios and on-site observations).[1]

**Student Writing: Minute Paper.**  The minute paper, a popular classroom assessment technique described by Angelo and Cross (1993), provides a snapshot of short-term student learning. For example, Eden Segal concluded a class discussion on the cultural and social functions of popular culture by asking the class, "What's one thing you learned from today's discussion?" The anonymous responses indicated that the students had listened well to the diversity of opinions in the class:

> That one person's hero can be another person's villain.

> I learned race is a littler bigger influence than I thought. Some people see Tiger Woods as a good influence but a lot of members of the black community don't think of him as a positive icon.

> I learned that Michael Jordan is a raceless icon. I never really considered this before, but it seems to have a lot of truth to it.

We interpreted this evidence of listening and awareness of differing opinions as students' readiness to think critically about their own positions. This enabled us to follow up with a journal prompt that carried them further in that direction.

**Student Reflective Writing: Journals.**  Weekly online journals have been a vital part of the AMST 498J experience. We design journal prompts that ask students to describe and analyze significant experiences and then follow up with probing questions to elicit deeper metacognition. The journal prompts nearly always emerge from a presentation or discussion in our weekly class sessions. Our aim is not only for students to learn from past experience but also to encourage them to begin recognizing their own learning moments without our prompting. Because the journal "conversation" includes only the student and the two instructors, it functions as a private mentoring session.

In recent versions of the course, we are delving more deeply into these learning moments. We asked students specifically to identify such moments: "In class this week we began to explore multiple forms of prose, document, and quantitative illiteracies. We also revealed some costs, including human ones. Did you have any epiphanies (the proverbial 'light bulb' or 'aha' moment)? As you view your experiences at the Boys and Girls Club through lenses of illiteracies, what do you see?" This prompt comes at a critical point in the semester when they have been tutoring for several weeks and we have also introduced the bulk of the content on literacy and the race and class demographics of literacy in America. In the journals, we look for evidence that the student can connect the more abstract facts and figures from the readings and lecture with their own firsthand experiences with high school students who are performing several years below grade level in reading and math. In addition, we hope that they exhibit an understanding of the personal implications of illiteracy for the student they are tutoring. These journal entries are typical of those who "get it":

> So far, in my experiences at [the high school], I have encountered a lot of students who may have a form of "prose illiteracy." For example, I tutored a ninth grader during my second week there (T). I had noticed that she was able to read the words on the page fine. However, she couldn't comprehend the words she was reading, or much less, answer any of the general questions that followed the passage. And because of this, she was losing focus. I strongly feel that literacy goes beyond just being able to read words. But being able to apply those words into everyday life [and] understand what you read, I feel, is vital. I feel that if a child has trouble comprehending what he/she is reading, then he/she must also have trouble focusing in on instructions on exams, etc., in school. Here illiteracy can be directly related to poor academic skills.

> What really caught me off guard was that K was *completely* clueless as to how to solve any of the problems. He didn't know whether to use addition, subtraction, multiplication, or division. Even after doing a couple of problems and having another problem almost exactly the same, he couldn't do it. He had no problem-solving skills! Because I do not know that much about K or his educational past, I do not know if his illiteracy is caused by a learning disability, not caring, or ineffective teaching, but he definitely needs those skills in life and does not have them.

It is rare that any student falls short of this expectation, since the literacy problems among the high school students is painfully obvious, but when anyone has trouble making the connection, a probing question from the instructor usually results in a productive exchange. In short, for the students, the journals function as a channel for reflective self-assessment, supported by instructor comments, which may encourage, probe, praise, or challenge their thinking. Taken in concert, the journals from the entire class for a given week help us adjust the direction and pace of the course.

**Student Reflective Writing: Portfolios.** The final project in AMST 498J is an electronic portfolio of essays and selected journal entries, intended to offer students the opportunity to select, integrate, and showcase their learning over the course of the semester. These are used for summative assessment of the students and for course assessment, to help us determine what works and what doesn't. We use the KEEP Toolkit, a free Web-based presentation tool developed by the Knowledge Media Laboratory of the Carnegie Foundation for the Advancement of Teaching for creating and sharing the portfolios. Students are required to include an introduction, one essay about what they learned through online discussions about a topic related to popular culture or literacy, one essay using excerpts from their journals to demonstrate learning, one essay on a topic of their choice, and a conclusion.

The creation of the final portfolio overlaps with the last two class meetings and the last journal prompt of the semester, both of which are intentionally crafted to focus their attention on making their own learning evident. The penultimate class meeting is a presentation by the instructors and undergraduate research assistant currently working on the project. In this session we take the students "behind the curtain" to reveal the pedagogical theory and research that supports AMST 498J and discuss our current research into multicultural teaching. The journal prompt that week builds on that foundation, asking, "What have you learned this semester . . . that you believe will stay with you after the semester ends and you're on to the next thing?" The responses to this prompt are used to sort the class into groups for a "fishbowl" activity in the final class, where students are asked to share with the entire group one thing they learned this semester and to listen carefully to the testimony of others. This practice of informing them about our research, eliciting their learning reflections, and providing a forum for sharing those reflections has served to transition them very effectively into the creation of the final portfolio.

## Mapping Point A and Point B

As indicated earlier, our biggest challenge has been to identify how far students have "traveled" during the semester in terms of multicultural learning. Knowing where they started, which we began to refer to in shorthand as "point A," seemed to be central to a fair assessment at the end of the course, to which we referred as "point B." After all, it would hardly be fair to reward a student for a level of understanding acquired a year ago in a different class or to fail to recognize the growth in a student who had moved from a position of resentment and hostility to one of uncertainty about his earlier views. Realistically, establishing point A is complicated by students' hesitation to be honest about perspectives or expectations, particularly regarding controversial subjects such as race and class. Most college students have mastered the art of saying what they believe teachers want to hear about racism and inequality. Not until a trusting relationship is established are most of us comfortable exploring where our views fail to match socially appropriate language. The opportunity to revisit their earlier journal posts and provide additional context, explanation, or even contradiction in the final portfolio has proved especially valuable for the students as well as the instructors.

In the final portfolio, most of the students are able to identify and describe their beliefs or expectations at the beginning of the course, and nearly all admit to having been either naive or disingenuous in their initial journals. Some had seen themselves as "miracle workers," like the transformative teachers in Hollywood's educational mythology. Often these students did not anticipate the complexity of the task or the possibility that they might be transformed by their young charges:

> In a journal entry I posted after my second week of tutoring I said, "He is still not really planning for his future, at least grades-wise, but hopefully over the next few weeks I can make him realize how the decisions he makes today are going to be affecting the rest of his life." I look back on this and see a lot of good intention in this statement; however, I now realize that it can take more than a few short weeks to change a person's outlook on life.

> I thought that this experience working at Northwestern was not really going to impact me or teach me much that I did not already know about working with kids in a diverse environment. . . . Now at point B I am even more aware of the kinds of experiences I need to continue to have in order to grow and learn about myself in diverse situations.

Others had harbored feelings of fear and uneasiness, expecting the high school students to be hostile and unwelcoming:

> I had to overcome several challenges, especially in the first couple of weeks. The biggest challenge I faced was actually going to the school. The first week the situation was slightly uncomfortable because I felt like I was in the minority as a white college-aged male.

> My assumptions were that high school kids would not be interested in receiving help and that it would be difficult to connect with them, which turned out not to be the case at all. In fact almost all the students were actually very open to making those emotional connections when they saw that we had a genuine interest in their lives and in helping them succeed.

NEW DIRECTIONS FOR TEACHING AND LEARNING • DOI: 10.1002/tl

From a multicultural perspective, persons with a minority or "other" status might differ from majority counterparts in the appropriateness of certain ends. For example, using Banks's stages of cultural identity (2004), a teacher might aim to lead all students toward cultural identity clarification but find that members of a dominant group retreat to cultural psychological captivity after internalizing negative beliefs about privilege. Banks's model also posits multicultural learning as linear. Our observation is that students may move back and forth among Banks's stages, skip stages, or be at different stages depending on the aspect of difference involved. An example of this last position would be an African American student who is quite comfortable and effective tutoring African Americans but less so in interactions with Latino students or recent immigrants from Africa.

> I wanted to challenge myself by stepping outside of my comfortable box and tutor one of the Hispanic kids and to get to know them better. . . . I was ashamed that I was hesitant to help due to the fear of not knowing their culture, understanding them, or them understanding me.

In fact, it is the enormous diversity in the self-reported learning among African American students who took the course that confirmed our decision to use qualitative, interpretive methods in our research:

> I thought I would have nothing in common with these kids because we grew up very differently. I grew up in farm country Connecticut, and these kids grew up in the outskirts of two major cities, Washington, D.C., and Baltimore. However, in the grand scheme of things, I found out that kids pretty much act the same way regardless of where they are from. I found that the students I tutored reminded me of how I acted when I was their age.

> In many ways, I have more in common with the white person who is aware of racial inequality but is too busy living their comfortable life to truly appreciate the enormity of the problem. In fact, I think my disengagement with racial issues was even worse. As a black woman, I was missing the "white guilt" that so often spurs privileged white folks to action.

As a result, we have adopted the position that for students (and perhaps for anyone else) to identify point A and then describe their own departure from that point evidences positive learning. Only apathy or feelings of persecution would be considered negative outcomes, and fortunately, we have not had to contend with either in the course so far.

The identification and articulation of point B is complicated not only by the various starting and ending points but also by the complex power dynamic that suggests how we should think and behave culturally. This is commonly expressed by our students as holding "politically correct" opinions and beliefs. So far we have not invented a performance detector that reveals when a student response is insincere. The best we can do is focus on the interpretation of evidence such as student writing and behavior.

Christina Totino has studied several semesters' worth of portfolios and selected journals, doing a close reading of the ways that students describe their experiences at the beginning, middle, and end of the course. She found that prior service-learning or tutoring experience had little effect on the students' inclination to mention race in their early journals. The race of the tutors, however, played a role in their level of comfort talking about race, with students of color more likely to describe the high school students as being of a particular race, whereas white students used nonracial descriptors ("tall" or "quiet," for example). By the end of the semester, most students were willing to articulate their initial assumptions about race and class, even when those assumptions had been negative. In their final portfolios or journals, most students had reevaluated the initial assumptions they made about the high school students, based on race or class. She also found a high degree of consistency between what the students articulated in the "private" journal conversations and the public portfolios. Because the portfolios are based on the journals, this is not surprising. Future research will focus on "negative" journal entries and the extent to which they are referenced later in the portfolio.

## Observation of Student Behavior

One of the most valuable methods of assessing the sincerity of student learning claims has been direct observation of their behavior at the service-learning site. Each section of the course has one or two undergraduate teaching assistants whose serves as mentor, information resource, and observer. It is in this last role that they are able to verify or contradict students' descriptions of events and interactions and to provide another perspective on student self-assessments. We ask all the students, in one of their journals, to summarize the most significant lesson learned and to provide experiential evidence that supports their accounts. They are informed that these journal entries, unlike all the others, will be shared with their undergraduate teaching assistants for verification. During our weekly team meeting, we review these entries with the undergraduate teaching assistants, who can corroborate or contradict the students' reports, based on their own observation. The results have been more than satisfactory. Not only have the entries been more nuanced and complicated, but we have been able to identify students who seem to be less than candid and challenge their self-assessments. For example, a tutor reported having established a close bond with a specific high school student over the course of the semester; however, her teaching assistant's tutoring records showed that she had worked with the student only a few times, usually in group situations. Ideally, this reality check results in constructive feedback to the student, in time to produce altered behavior. It is astonishing to us that students who are inclined to "embellish" their on-site accomplishments seem to forget that they are being observed.

## Conclusion

Teaching—and assessing learning—about diversity through service-learning is full of challenges, especially if the learning goals are affective. The teacher has no good way of knowing exactly where the starting point is for each student. The student may only know where the starting point was once he or she has moved beyond it and sees it in retrospect. Students may be reluctant to share or analyze negative feelings or experiences. They may even attempt to perform "desirable" learning. It may be difficult to gauge affective learning under these circumstances, but it is not impossible. Careful use of student writing and observation, combined with on-site observation, can help the instructors—and the students themselves—capture epiphanies and connect experience and reflection to document new learning.

## Note

1. All quotations from AMST 498J student journals and portfolios are from the 2005–06 academic year and are used with the students' permission. All names are pseudonyms.

## References

Angelo, T. A., and Cross, K. P. *Classroom Assessment Techniques: A Handbook for College Teachers.* San Francisco: Jossey-Bass, 1993.
Banks, J. A. "Teaching for Social Justice, Diversity, and Citizenship in a Global World." *Educational Forum,* 2004, *68,* 296–305.
Gelmon, S. B., and others. *Assessing Service-Learning and Civic Engagement: Principles and Techniques.* Providence, R.I.: Campus Compact, 2001.

## Additional Resources

Boyle-Baise, M. *Multicultural Service Learning: Educating Teachers in Diverse Communities.* New York: Teachers College Press, 2002.
National Service-Learning Clearinghouse. "Assessment and Evaluation in Service-Learning." http://www.servicelearning.org/nslc/bib_archive/index.php. Accessed May 30, 2007.

*JO B. PAOLETTI is an associate professor in American studies at the University of Maryland, College Park.*

*EDEN SEGAL is a doctoral candidate in educational policy and leadership at the University of Maryland, College Park.*

*CHRISTINA TOTINO is an undergraduate history major at the University of Maryland, College Park.*

# 7

*The authors describe the structure and impact of faculty-led intercultural field placements involving diverse groups of students.*

# New Learning and Teaching from Where You've Been: The Global Intercultural Experience for Undergraduates

*A. T. Miller, Edith Fernández*

When we began to design the Global Intercultural Experience for Undergraduates (GIEU) at the University of Michigan, we were looking to create a comprehensive program that would have a profound impact on the way students learned at the university and on the way faculty approached their students and taught. This was in addition to the mandate to both broaden and increase the level of "global" education at the university and to make sure that such a program drew in a far more diverse range of students and faculty than past efforts at experiential, community, or international learning. We wanted to be sure that our program had a positive impact on the community sites that were involved and a lasting impact on campus as well, building real and recognized skills among the student and faculty participants. All of these goals demanded a rigorous assessment regime and a complex and integrated set of activities that would build and develop from each other around a set of central field experiences.

## Program Description

Each year GIEU funds eight to twelve faculty-proposed projects at sites both domestic and international. Each group is diverse and includes ten to fourteen undergraduates (GIEU student scholars) from across the university,

NEW DIRECTIONS FOR TEACHING AND LEARNING, no. 111, Fall 2007 © Wiley Periodicals, Inc.
Published online in Wiley InterScience (www.interscience.wiley.com) • DOI: 10.1002/tl.286

along with one or two faculty members (GIEU teaching fellows). The groups visit culturally rich sites for three or four weeks during the summer months. For GIEU student scholars, this summer experience is a paid internship involving them with diverse peers in close local interactions. For the GIEU teaching fellows, it provides a stipend and the opportunity to work in creative and innovative ways with an interdisciplinary undergraduate team in the field. A wrap-around course for the students that begins in late February and ends in late September is complemented by a faculty seminar for all of the instructors. Prior to that, selection processes for both faculty proposals and student participants culminate in a December matching event at which the students selected for GIEU are matched with the GIEU experiences that will be offered over the coming summer. Because our emphasis is on intercultural learning, we try to deemphasize recruitment for particular field programs and encourage all participants to be open to both the domestic and international sites that might be available. The skills, habits of mind and behavior, openness, experiences, cooperation, and adaptability of both the students and the faculty members are cultivated through various exercises, community activities, reflective journaling, and small-team discussions.

GIEU is designed to have a positive and very broad impact on campus far beyond the individual participants. Faculty proposals must describe how the learning will come back to campus, and programs in intergroup relations and the Student Activities and Leadership office, along with the service-learning center, are involved in various phases of GIEU. Field sites change each year in order to permit new collaborations and a wider influence across campus. The students are drawn mostly from the first- and second-year classes so that their experiences can influence the activities they pursue during their remaining years on campus. Faculty may repeat the program once, although particular field experiences might repeat more than that if led by different faculty members. This allows academic departments and programs to cultivate a site or experience and develop it, with the hope that some will come to stand on their own outside of GIEU, as has already happened in a few cases.

The participants in GIEU over the years have been over half students of color, and the same has been true of the faculty participants. Students have come from all of our schools and colleges with undergraduate programs, and faculty have come from these units as well as from schools and colleges that offer only graduate degrees. Our most senior faculty (including a former university president) have participated, along with lecturers and research scientists. GIEU draws international and domestic students and faculty, both cosmopolitan and those lacking intercultural experience. Each year between 30 and 40 percent of GIEU students are on university-recognized financial aid, and we make a special outreach to first-generation college students, students in intensive academic programs (such as engineering or nursing) that have little space for electives, students of color, and male students, all of whom tend not to participate in experiential field learning programs. The course is offered as a university course so that the credit may be used in any major or college, and a GIEU experience meets some of the global, diversity, or field requirements for several academic programs. It also often feeds directly into our study-abroad, undergraduate research, service-learning, leadership, and intergroup relations programs.

## Program Evaluation Design

Among the undergraduates we attempt to cultivate, measure, and study something that we are calling "global perspective," informed by the work of Kegan (1994) on mental organization and self-authorship, King and Baxter Magolda (2005) on intercultural maturity, and Bennett (2004) on intercultural sensitivity. We are quite intentionally stepping away from models of cultural or intercultural competence, which often emphasize the trifecta of knowledge, skills, and actions. We see ourselves as preparing both our students and our faculty for the unfamiliar, for work with strangers, for the ability to hit the ground running in places not their own and embrace new understandings with abilities to learn and act appropriately in context. Such personal capacity must be grounded in a mental perspective, an internal resource to be drawn on in habits of mind, rather than particular learned responses.

The concept of a global perspective is a complex one involving the ability to engage in critical self-reflection and to navigate an intercultural setting while acting in culturally sensitive and informed ways. By contrast, competence often implies focusing on the demonstration of skills per se, without any demonstrated self-awareness or reflection. Exploring someone's perspective, however, requires examining the underlying attitudes, beliefs, and cognitive structure that form the basis for using one's knowledge and skills. This approach includes components of the cognitive, interpersonal, and intrapersonal domains of development.

We draw on Kegan's holistic approach to these three domains (1994) to frame a global perspective as an important student learning outcome. King and Baxter Magolda (2005) built on this work to conceptualize how attention to each of these three areas can develop a mature capacity to consciously shift perspectives and behaviors into an alternative cultural worldview and to use multiple cultural frames. Individuals at the mature intrapersonal level of development have the capacity to create an internal self that openly engages challenges to one's views and beliefs and considers social identities (race, class, gender, and so on) in global and national contexts. Such individuals have the capacity to engage in meaningful reciprocal relationships with diverse others that are grounded in an understanding of, and appreciation for, human differences. Bennett (2004) studied the way people construe cultural difference and the varying kinds of development that accompany different constructions and termed this development "intercultural sensitivity." He proposes the Developmental Model of Intercultural Sensitivity, which recognizes that an increase in cultural awareness is accompanied by the development of empathy and improved cognitive sophistication. As a person's ability to understand differences increases, so does his or her ability to negotiate a variety of worldviews, a clear developmental marker. His continuum moves from stages defined as ethnocentric to those identified as ethnorelative.

In the GIEU program, an integrated global perspective is desirable because it helps one engage in critical consciousness and function at the optimal level of cultural sensitivity, continuous learning, and maturity to face the challenges and pressures of a multicultural environment and benefit from its opportunities. Our model for such a perspective includes four dimensions: (1) preferences for thinking and interacting, (2) intercultural relations, (3) intrapersonal awareness, and (4) global awareness. These dimensions are measured along a continuum from "monocultural global perspective" at the lower end to "integrated global perspective" at the higher end. Measures include the extent of one's ability to adopt others' perspectives, the degree to which one prefers complex explanations of behavior, the extent to which one seeks interactions with those different from oneself, one's awareness of the array of components that constitute one's own identity and how they affect others in various cultural contexts, and the degree of one's openness to and understanding of cross-cultural differences.

## Program Impact

We have collected extensive data on the program in the first five years and have learned a great deal about what our faculty and students are getting out of this heavily integrated intercultural program. At the orientation and debriefing sessions, students fill out a pre- and post-field-experience survey designed by one of the authors (Fernández, 2006). Both before and after their field experience, faculty take the Intercultural Development Inventory, a fifty-item psychometric instrument developed by Hammer (1998), which measures six areas of Bennett's original Developmental Model of Intercultural Sensitivity (1993). We also interview faculty immediately after the project and then one year later to find out what impact the experience has had on their teaching and research. The students keep reflective journals throughout the experience, from which we (with their permission) and they (on our behalf) draw qualitative data. They write final essays at the end of the experience and are interviewed at graduation, often two to three years after they have participated in the GIEU program. We also seek evidence from or about the local field partners to assess if we are meeting our goal of benefiting these communities as much as we do our university constituents.

Overall, our quantitative measures show that on average, students and faculty show a greater interest and willingness to be involved in and face situations of cultural difference and conflict. Both groups also saw a corresponding drop in assertions of confidence in personal ability and knowledge in these areas.

The cognitive items include nine that focus on attributional complexity (for example, "I think a lot about the influence society has on other people") and six that examine perspective taking ("I try to look at everybody's side of a disagreement"). Results indicate that students do not change much on these scales. For example, both before and after the experiences, they strongly agree with the statement about society's influence on other people, and they "agree somewhat" with the statement about trying to look at all points of view.

Interpersonal items include fourteen on global awareness (for example, "I often think about what I have in common with other people in the world") and eight on intergroup anxiety (reaction to "being laughed at for a minor mistake"), while the intrapersonal scale has six items ("I am aware of how people outside my own culture respond to my social identity"). Students show slight incremental growth on these items, but given the size of our sample and the short duration of the program, the growth has significance.

Our qualitative measures provide a much clearer sense of the long-term impact of the GIEU. Analysis of faculty writing and interviews reveal that GIEU has stimulated the self-awareness of our faculty teaching fellows as intercultural learners and brought them to value the importance of reflection for students as well as themselves. They show an enthusiasm for the world as an experiential classroom and speak directly of the challenges of working with students' various developmental levels and group dynamics. They gain new insights for curriculum and research and are actively sharing these insights with colleagues, and they have gained confidence in diverse undergraduate ability. Here are some comments from faculty participants:

> I learned a tremendous amount about globalization and diversity. The growth of students was amazing, as was seeing that it was really possible. It was a true transformation. [It had] a big impact [on curriculum], giving me a battery of examples and cases. Very rich. (professor of sociology)

> I have more tools to deal with these sorts of situations [conflict among diverse students], and the only resource in my life for this has been GIEU. (lecturer in Romance languages)

> I am going to use [what I learned] in my training of instructors, especially non-U.S. instructors, about issues of diversity. (lecturer in Romance languages)

> I have a new capacity to build an intercultural team between students. (instructor in women's studies and psychology)

> I learned lots about the need to reflect on cultural experiences and learn about students and how they learn, about their limits and lack of experience. (professor of history)

Student interviews, journals, and essays reveal common themes of examining their personal identities and stretching themselves while learning from group interactions, understanding privilege, and recognizing the limits of their own knowledge. Our students often reconnect to their field experience and host peoples through additional academic projects at the University of Michigan, exploring multiple identities and looking for additional opportunities. In many instances, GIEU serves as a gateway to intercultural career paths. The full impact of the program is clear in the following quotes taken from open-ended surveys conducted when the students graduate, usually two to three years after their participation in GIEU:

> The GIEU program has definitely had an impact on my undergraduate years. Upon returning from my field site, I became involved with Project Community, a service-learning course. . . . I used my own experiences as the basis for a lesson plan that I designed. I then traveled to various schools throughout the metropolitan area and presented my lesson to different classes. In addition, I served as a member of the Detroit Project planning team this past year. My involvement with GIEU furthered my interest in service-learning opportunities and challenged me to think critically about my surroundings. (2004 participant)

> I can say without a doubt that the three weeks I spent . . . in the summer of 2002 were among the most influential experiences of my time here at the university. Following the trip I added Latin American and Caribbean studies as a second major, studied for five months at the University of the Americas in Puebla, Mexico, and spent a month doing archival research in Cuba for my history thesis. (2002 participant)

> My experience . . . with GIEU started me on a whole new and unexpected path. I changed my major after that experience, I did my senior thesis research back in the same town that I had [visited] with GIEU, I have stayed in very close communication with [the faculty], and I am actually employed by them as a translator right now. I cannot imagine what my college experience would have been like without . . . GIEU. (2004 participant)

One significant finding is that the impact of GIEU experiences increases over time for both students and faculty. For example, we discovered that our program was producing leadership for existing and new campus organizations that cross traditional student enclaves and develop broader networks of students. This outcome was not an initial goal of the program but has become increasingly evident as we gain insights from our graduation and long-term surveys. Similarly, faculty found that their involvement in GIEU had broader and unexpected consequences on their own development along the intercultural sensitivity spectrum. The GIEU grants and experiences have ended up affecting faculty teaching in courses on campus, their research questions and approaches, their engagement and insight into the lives and development of undergraduates, and their openness to intercultural, experiential, and interdisciplinary teaching and learning. Faculty often express appreciative surprise at the capacities of undergraduates, particularly in working with students from diverse majors, often far outside their fields of expertise.

## Explanation of Impact

Through regression analysis we have determined that the aspects of the program that have more immediate impact are the reflective journals, the close interactions with faculty, and the diverse teams. In particular, students immediately appreciate and continually comment on how they become close to and work with people they would otherwise never meet. These same factors have a strong impact on faculty. We also examined the ways in which our program has differing effects on different types of students and faculty, with some of the biggest changes happening for the students most typical of the university (those from higher-income suburban backgrounds) and faculty with the most typical profiles (those who are most strongly discipline-focused). Because these are the groups least likely to find themselves in intercultural interactions on campus, it is not surprising that they are the most strongly affected by participation in an intercultural program. For other groups, GIEU also has an impact on attitudes and perspectives, though not as great. Participation in GIEU is, however, more likely to lead members of these groups (as opposed to the more "typical" group) to pursue opportunities on campus that build on their work in the program.

When we distinguish between the kinds of activities students engage in during particular field experiences, we find that the closer the interactions are with local constituents—for example, lodging with a local family—and the more the experience produces "intercultural anxiety" during field site activities, the greater the growth in developing an integrated global perspective. The student outcomes that showed complex thinking in intercultural situations were also enhanced by structured and reflective peer interactions across difference mediated by faculty members to acknowledge, surface, and process conflict. Service-learning activities on site were also significant in promoting cross-cultural interactions and learning, mainly because they provided context and purpose to the presence of outsiders at particular field sites. Students achieved the most positive learning outcomes and experienced the most development along the continuum when they were engaged in intimate interactions across lines of religion, participated in cultural rituals and events, and had opportunities for reflection with peers and faculty. This type of development deepened and was enhanced after students returned, as time and additional experiences offered further contexts for learning.

The outcomes for faculty were similarly enhanced by close interaction at the field site, reflection done together with the students, and the opportunity to compare outcomes with other faculty members engaged in similar projects. One year after the experience, these effects were enhanced, and insights were often greater than at the immediate debriefings and surveys. Faculty were often eager to repeat the experience a year or two later, to build on the insights gained and to encourage others to propose projects.

The mix of qualitative and quantitative assessment measures, both immediate and long-term, have been essential to understanding and refining GIEU. The results indicate that the program not only generates robust immediate results but also provides a set of experiences and tools that gain strength as participants find more and diverse contexts in which to apply their new knowledge and habits of mind. Some aspects of the program that generate initial resistance—such as administering cultural sensitivity measures to faculty members, pushing students into situations of intercultural anxiety, or expecting both to reflect frankly and in one another's presence—have all proved especially productive.

We recognize that there is a strong self-selection effect to programs like this that are competitive on both a faculty and a student level. We have not been able to survey as extensively a control group that has not been exposed to the GIEU program, but we have been able to compare between the various forty-five field experiences offered over the first five years of the program to discover the attributes that have the strongest positive outcomes. We trust that those data are valuable to individuals responsible for planning experiential higher education field activities in diverse communities.

## References

Bennett, M. J. "Becoming Interculturally Competent." In J. Wurzel (ed.), *Toward Multiculturalism: A Reader in Multicultural Education* (2nd ed.). Newton, Mass.: Intercultural Resource Corp., 2004.

Bennett, M. J. "Towards Ethnorelativism: A Developmental Model of Intercultural Sensitivity." In M. Paige (ed.), *Education for the Intercultural Experience*. Yarmouth, Maine: Intercultural Press, 1993.

Fernández, E. "Developing a Global Perspective During a Study-Term Abroad." Ph.D. diss., University of Michigan, 2006.

Hammer, M. R. "A Measure of Intercultural Sensitivity: The Intercultural Development Inventory." In S. Fowler and M. Fowler (eds.), *The Intercultural Sourcebook*, Vol. 2. Yarmouth, Maine: Intercultural Press, 1998.

Kegan, R. *In over Our Heads: The Mental Demands of Modern Life*. Cambridge, Mass.: Harvard University Press, 1994.

King, P. M., and Baxter Magolda, M. B. "A Developmental Model of Intercultural Maturity." *Journal of College Student Development*, 2005, 46(6), 571–592.

A. T. MILLER *is coordinator of multicultural teaching and learning at the Center for Research on Learning and Teaching and director of the Global Intercultural Experiences for Undergraduates Program at the University of Michigan.*

EDITH FERNÁNDEZ *is director of the Student Development Center and the Women's Resource Center at the University of Texas–El Paso.*

**8**

*The authors describe three initiatives designed to increase the academic achievement and retention of historically underrepresented students (including females and under-represented students of color) in engineering.*

# Diversity and Retention in Engineering

*Cinda-Sue G. Davis, Cynthia J. Finelli*

The engineer of the twenty-first century will compete in an increasingly global environment and face an expanding array of problems in the business sector as well as the social sector. To meet these challenges, the U.S. engineering education enterprise must produce graduates who are not only technically proficient but also diverse in terms of background, culture, outlook, and approach. Several national committees and reports have emphasized the critical importance of a diverse student and workforce population in the science, technology, engineering, and mathematics (STEM) fields (BEST, 2004a; 2004b; Chubin, May, and Babco, 2005; National Academy of Engineering, 2006; Wulf, 1998). Yet groups that have historically been underrepresented, particularly females and underrepresented students of color, are still not pursuing engineering degrees in proportion to their representation in the general public, despite decades of programs and interventions. Recent efforts at the University of Michigan (U-M), combining both curricular and cocurricular initiatives, offer some promising outcomes in terms of student academic achievement and retention. Three such initiatives are outlined in this chapter: (1) providing an opportunity for undergraduates to participate in research, (2) including service-learning in the first-year curriculum, and (3) introducing real-world context in a first-year computing course.

## Undergraduate Research

Initially designed in 1989 as a retention program for historically underrepresented students, the Undergraduate Research Opportunity Program (UROP) was soon expanded to include all interested students in 1992.

NEW DIRECTIONS FOR TEACHING AND LEARNING, no. 111, Fall 2007 © Wiley Periodicals, Inc.
Published online in Wiley InterScience (www.interscience.wiley.com) • DOI: 10.1002/tl.287

Today approximately twelve hundred first- and second-year students participate annually in research projects for work-study financial aid or academic credit with U-M faculty. Through the program, UROP students meet regularly with peer advisors who are upper-division UROP alumni, and UROP students are intentionally integrated into the university's core academic mission. Projects in which UROP students participate range from Physics of Spacecraft Propulsion: Analytical Modeling and Computer Simulation to Reception and Interpretation of the Films of Akira Kurosawa. Students participate in all aspects of the research enterprise, including literature searches, laboratory experimentation, and research presentations. Although UROP serves students in all of U-M's undergraduate schools and colleges, demand for positions is always great among engineering students.

Several assessment and evaluation efforts suggest that UROP participation positively influences academic achievement and retention, the extent of student participation in the educational experience, and participation in postgraduate activities related to academics. However, the findings vary by race or ethnicity, gender, and other student characteristics (Gregerman, 1999; Hathaway, Nagda, and Gregerman, 2002; Nagda and others, 1998).

One study involved a longitudinal retention analysis of 1,280 students, with UROP students carefully matched to non-UROP students who had applied to the program but who had not been accepted (Nagda and others, 1998). Overall, there was a positive (but nonsignificant) effect of UROP participation on retention. This effect was strongest for African American students: in that population, retention for UROP students was 90 percent, versus 82 percent for the control group. UROP participation also has a slight differential effect on retention rates for low-achieving students (88 percent versus 86 percent). Again, this effect was strongest for African American students (85 percent versus 73 percent).

Focus group data and an alumni survey were analyzed in a separate study to identify further benefits of the program (Hathaway, Nagda, and Gregerman, 2002). The focus group data indicated that UROP students tend to be more proactive than non-UROP students. They are more likely than non-UROP students to initiate activity with people, to anticipate problems before they arise, to act before being acted on, and to seek out help from individuals. In addition, UROP students are more likely to discuss how they interact with the academic environment and are more likely to see faculty, staff, and others as positive influences on their academic experiences. The alumni study (in which 291 UROP and non-UROP graduates responded to a survey about postgraduate educational pursuit and activities) found that students who participate in undergraduate research (UROP or other research) are significantly more likely to pursue postgraduate education (medical, law, or doctoral degrees) than control students. However, no differences by race or ethnicity in postgraduate educational pursuit were observed.

NEW DIRECTIONS FOR TEACHING AND LEARNING • DOI: 10.1002/tl

Although the research findings cited previously are for all university UROP participants (including engineering students), the UROP program also undertook an engineering study in which retention for 5,228 undergraduate students who majored in engineering between 1998 and 2002 was compared for 857 UROP students and for 4,371 non-UROP students (Hathaway, 2003). Although retention for UROP and non-UROP students was not significantly different overall (83 percent and 81 percent retention for UROP and non-UROP, respectively), disaggregation of the data by race and gender yielded interesting results. For underrepresented students of color, retention is significantly higher for UROP than non-UROP students (77 percent versus 65 percent). This is also true for Asian and Asian American students (91 percent versus 87 percent), but there is no significant effect of UROP participation for white students. Similarly, three-way ANOVA comparison of UROP participation, ethnicity, and gender is also significant ($p < .001$), indicating a different impact of UROP by gender and ethnicity (see Table 8.1). In particular, UROP has the greatest impact on retention for female underrepresented students of color (81 percent versus 60 percent), followed by Asian and Asian American males (94 percent versus 86 percent) and male underrepresented students of color (76 percent versus 68 percent).

## Service-Learning

A second initiative at U-M involved introducing service-learning into the first-year curriculum. Since the mid-1900s, traditional undergraduate engineering education has focused on teaching specialized technical knowledge to students for the purpose of solving challenging problems. As a result, engineers of the last half-century have been highly technically trained but have often lacked professional skills, communication skills, and the broad education necessary to understand their impact in a global and social context (National Academy of Engineering, 2004). A service-learning course is

**Table 8.1. Retention Rates (in percent) by UROP Participation, Ethnicity, and Gender: A Three-Way ANOVA Comparison**

| | | Males | | | Females | |
|---|---|---|---|---|---|---|
| Group | White | Asian and Asian American | Underrepresented Students of Color | White | Asian and Asian American | Underrepresented Students of Color |
| UROP | 87 | 94 | 76 | 74 | 87 | 81 |
| Non-UROP | 84 | 86 | 66 | 77 | 88 | 60 |

*Source:* Data from Hathaway, 2003; used with permission.

NEW DIRECTIONS FOR TEACHING AND LEARNING • DOI: 10.1002/tl

one way to address these curricular deficiencies and enhance social awareness in the engineering field (Coyle, Jamieson, and Oakes, 2006). Such a course includes three primary components: relevant and meaningful service in the community, enhanced academic learning, and purposeful civic learning (Howard, 2001).

There are many benefits to including a service-learning design project in the first-year engineering curriculum. First, it facilitates the development of professional skills in engineering students as they work in the community. Second, it brings active and reflective learning to students and has been shown to produce deeper understanding and better application of subject matter, increased ability to solve complex problems, and greater use of subject matter knowledge in analyzing a problem (Gallini and Moely, 2003; Tsang, 2000). Third, since historically underrepresented groups, including females and underrepresented students of color, often cite the ability to solve social problems as a prime reason for choosing a career in science or engineering (Astin and Sax, 1996; Seymour and Hewitt, 1997), service-learning allows these students the opportunity to apply their skills in a social setting. By revealing the human aspect of engineering and making it socially relevant from the outset of their education, service-learning has the potential to increase diversity within the profession.

In fall 2004, 114 first-year students elected a service-learning section of Engineering 100, an introductory engineering class (Meadows and Jarema, 2006). Teams of students participated in a design project to develop innovative, low-cost greenhouses for several local, underfunded public schools. The greenhouses served the needs of the community, provided yearlong growing potential to supplement standard food offerings in schools and community service facilities, and supported early plantings for local community gardens. Interestingly, approximately 35 percent of the students who enrolled in this service-learning section were females and 15 percent were underrepresented students of color, while averages for the incoming class were about 25 percent and 10 percent, respectively.

To assess the effectiveness of the course in enhancing students' social awareness and improving the relevance of the curriculum, student evaluations of the course were collected at the end of the term. In Table 8.2, data from three terms when the course was taught without a service-learning component (fall 2002, fall 2003, and winter 2004) are compared to the term when service-learning was introduced (fall 2004). The same instructor taught the course all four terms.

Student evaluations of the service-learning term were significantly higher ($p < .001$) than those during previous terms, indicating that service-learning resulted in a greater sense of satisfaction with the course and the instructor. These data also indicate that the course succeeded in enhancing students' social awareness and in making the curriculum more relevant by getting students to grapple with social and economic issues that can arise in real-life engineering.

NEW DIRECTIONS FOR TEACHING AND LEARNING • DOI: 10.1002/tl

**Table 8.2.  Median Values for Student Responses to Items Pertinent
to the Service-Learning Curriculum**

| | No Service-Learning Component | | Incorporating Service-Learning | |
|---|---|---|---|---|
| | Fall 2002 (n = 70) | Fall 2003 (n = 75) | Winter 2004 (n = 94) | Fall 2004 (n = 114) |
| Overall, this was an excellent course. | 3.7 | 3.7 | 3.8 | 4.6 |
| Overall, the instructor was an excellent teacher. | 4.1 | 3.9 | 4.0 | 4.7 |
| I learned a great deal from this course. | 3.7 | 3.9 | 3.7 | 4.4 |
| I had a strong desire to take this course. | 3.0 | 3.1 | 3.1 | 4.0 |
| This course helped me understand the rewards and challenges of being an engineer. | 3.9 | 3.9 | 3.9 | 4.5 |
| This course helped me understand the range of skills/disciplines needed in engineering. | 3.9 | 3.9 | 3.9 | 4.4 |
| This course helped me understand social and economic considerations in engineering. | 4.1 | 4.0 | 3.9 | 4.4 |
| I have a sense of pride and accomplishment as a result of completing my projects. | 3.9 | 3.9 | 3.9 | 4.6 |
| I have become more aware of the responsibilities engineers have as professionals. | 4.0 | 4.1 | 4.0 | 4.6 |
| I will think more carefully about engineering's impact on society because of this course. | 3.8 | 3.8 | 3.8 | 4.5 |

*Notes:* Student responses were on a 5-point Likert scale from 1 = strongly disagree to 5 = strongly
agree. The same instructor taught the course during all four terms.

*Source:* Meadows and Jarema, 2006; reprinted with permission.

## Real-World Context

Another initiative intended to increase the academic achievement of historically underrepresented students was to introduce real-world context
in the first-year computing course (Engineering 101). In particular, to decrease the achievement gap between underrepresented students of color
and others (white students and Asian and Asian American students) and
between females and males, a two-phase analysis was conducted. First, to
identify factors that help or hinder *all* students in the course, survey data
were collected during the first and eighth weeks of the fall 2003 term in

NEW DIRECTIONS FOR TEACHING AND LEARNING • DOI: 10.1002/tl

one Engineering 101 course. Of the 185 enrolled students, 64 percent (119) completed both surveys. Data suggested that many students did not perceive computer programming and algorithmic thinking as useful and important to their future as engineers and that this perception had a negative effect on their motivation to engage with the course material. This finding was especially a matter for concern because usefulness and importance are two dimensions of student motivation that have been shown to affect persistence and achievement (Pintrich and Zusho, 2002; Wigfield and Eccles, 2000).

The second phase of the initiative involved modifying Engineering 101 to change students' perception about the importance and usefulness of programming, thereby motivating students to engage with the course (Burn and Holloway, 2006). In fall 2004, the instructor modified the course by consistently emphasizing and demonstrating to students the role of algorithmic thinking and programming in the work of engineers. As much as possible, the weekly programming assignments were also placed within the context of current events, real-world technologies, or applications to improve society. Each week a significant amount of lecture time (occasionally a full day) was devoted to introducing the assignment, the ideas behind it, and its real-world context.

To evaluate the effect of deliberately emphasizing the importance of programming, students in both the modified course and a separate section serving as a quasi–control group completed surveys during the second and thirteenth weeks. The response rate for students completing both surveys was 43 percent in both the modified course and the control section (96 of 221 students in the modified course and 98 of 226 students in the control section). From the beginning of the course to the thirteenth week, responses to the statement "It is important that engineering majors learn to program (1 = strongly disagree . . . 4 = strongly agree)" diverged for the two groups. The control group's perception of the importance of learning to program decreased markedly (–0.42) from the second to the thirteenth week of the term, while the decrease was negligible (–0.18) in the modified course. This difference between the sections was statistically significant. Hence exposure to the intricacies of algorithmic thinking did not detract from students' sense of its relevance in the modified section as it did in the control group.

It was difficult to evaluate the effect of adding real-world context to weekly assignments because it was not possible to adjust for the different assignments in the control group. However, a comparison of student survey responses from the fall 2003 course (in which traditional assignments were used) and the modified fall 2004 course (in which real-world context was introduced) provides an interesting insight. Both courses were taught by the same instructor. In both sections, students were asked to respond to the statement "I can see/imagine how the ideas from this class will be applied in my future (1 = strongly disagree, . . . 5 = strongly agree)" at the second and thirteenth weeks. In the traditionally taught course, there was a statistically significant decrease (–0.50) in students' perceptions of how course ideas would apply in the future from the second to the thirteenth weeks, while in the modified course there was no statistically significant difference. This result suggests the intervention had a positive effect.

A comparison of class grades between the students in the fall 2003 and fall 2004 courses is also illuminating. The grade gap between female and male students of all races dropped from 0.42 in fall 2003 to 0.17 in fall 2004, while the gap between underrepresented students of color and other students dropped from 0.68 to 0.56. This change could be traced to both improved exam performance and improved homework performance; the difference was best explained by improved exam performance for females and by improved homework performance for underrepresented students of color.

## Discussion

The National Academy of Engineering publication *Educating the Engineer of 2020* (2005) eloquently described how the undergraduate engineering (and science and mathematics) learning environment is changing in this century. Among other things, engineering undergraduate education must deal with changing "student demographics, with greater diversity from the perspective of academic preparation, career aspirations, and ethnic background that require approaches to learning, teaching, and research designed intentionally to respect (and celebrate) this diversity" (p. 36). As Linda Katehi, former dean of the College of Engineering at Purdue, wrote, "The new engineering curriculum must take into account that in the future students will learn in a completely different way. Up to now, engineering schools have developed curricula by creating scenarios or predicting the problems we expect to face. In doing so, we have focused on knowledge rather than skills. . . . Engineers whose education is built from the bottom up cannot comprehend and address big problems. They get lost in irrelevant details" (pp. 153–154).

What is particularly exciting about the initiatives discussed in this chapter is how they are changing the way undergraduate engineering education is approached. Innovations designed to help female students and underrepresented students of color actually benefited *all* students and aligned the engineering undergraduate experience much more closely to the ideals described in *Educating the Engineer of 2020*. Social relevance, respecting diversity, and problem solving, in addition to knowledge, seeing the big picture, and identification with the profession, are all components vital to the education and future careers of engineers in this century. And all are important components of the efforts described in this chapter. Introducing undergraduate research experiences, service-learning opportunities, and social and professional relevance to the engineering curriculum can strengthen the education and success of all students.

## References

Astin, H. S., and Sax, L. J. "Developing Scientific Talent in Undergraduate Women." In Davis, C. S., and others (eds.), *The Equity Equation: Fostering the Advancement of Women in the Sciences, Mathematics, and Engineering.* San Francisco: Jossey-Bass, 1996.

BEST: Building Engineering and Science Talent. *A Bridge for All: Higher Education Design Principles to Broaden Participation in Science, Technology, Engineering, and Mathematics.* San Diego, Calif.: BEST, 2004a.

BEST: Building Engineering and Science Talent. *The Talent Imperative: Diversifying America's Science and Engineering Workforce.* San Diego, Calif.: BEST, 2004b.

Burn, H., and Holloway, J. "Why Should I Care? Student Motivation in an Introductory Programming Course." *Proceedings of the ASEE Annual Conference and Exposition, Chicago,* 2006. (CD-ROM)

Chubin, D. E., May, G. S., and Babco, E. L. "Diversifying the Engineering Workforce." *Journal of Engineering Education,* 2005, *94*(1), 73–86.

Coyle, E. J., Jamieson, L. H., and Oakes, W. C. "Integrating Engineering Education and Community Service: Themes for the Future of Engineering Education." *Journal of Engineering Education,* 2006, *95*(1), 7–11.

Gallini, S. M., & Moely, B. E. "Service-Learning and Engagement, Academic Challenge, and Retention." *Michigan Journal of Community Service Learning,* 2003, *10*(1), 5–14.

Gregerman, S. R. "Improving the Academic Success of Diverse Students Through Undergraduate Research." *Council on Undergraduate Research Quarterly,* 1999, *20*(2), 54–59.

Hathaway, R. S. "UROP Engineering Retention Analyses: UROP and Non-UROP Engineering Retention Comparison." Unpublished report, University of Michigan, 2003.

Hathaway, R. S., Nagda, B. A., and Gregerman, S. R. "The Relationship of Undergraduate Research Participation to Graduate and Professional Educational Pursuit: An Empirical Study." *Journal of College Student Development,* 2002, *43*(5), 614–631.

Howard, J. *Service Learning Course Design Workbook: Companion Volume to Michigan Journal of Community Service Learning.* Ann Arbor: OCSL Press, University of Michigan, 2001.

Meadows, L., and Jarema, S. "An Evaluation of the Impact of a Service-Learning Project in a Required First-Year Engineering Course." *Proceedings of the ASEE Annual Conference and Exposition, Chicago,* 2006. (CD-ROM)

Nagda, B. A., and others. "Undergraduate Student-Faculty Research Partnerships Affect Student Retention." *Review of Higher Education,* 1998, *22*(1), 55–72.

National Academy of Engineering. *The Engineer of 2020: Visions of Engineering in the New Century.* Washington, D.C.: National Academies Press, 2004.

National Academy of Engineering. *Educating the Engineer of 2020: Adapting Engineering Education to the New Century.* Washington, D.C.: National Academies Press, 2005.

National Academy of Engineering. *Rising Above the Gathering Storm: Energizing and Employing America for a Brighter Economic Future.* Washington, D.C.: National Academies Press, 2006.

Pintrich, P., and Zusho, A. "Student Motivation and Self-Regulated Learning in the College Classroom." In J. C. Smart and W. G. Tierney (eds.), *Higher Education: Handbook of Theory and Research.* Boston: Kluwer, 2002.

Seymour, E., and Hewitt, N. *Talking About Leaving: Why Undergraduates Leave the Sciences.* Boulder, Colo.: Westview Press, 1997.

Tsang, E. (ed.). *Projects That Matter: Concepts and Models for Service Learning in Engineering,* Vol. 14. Washington, D.C.: American Association for Higher Education, 2000.

Wigfield, A., and Eccles, J. S. "Expectancy-Value Theory of Motivation." *Contemporary Educational Psychology,* 2000, 25(1), 68–81.
Wulf, W. A. "The Urgency of Engineering Education Reform." *Bridge,* 1998, 28(1), 1–7.

CINDA-SUE G. DAVIS *is director of the Women in Science and Engineering Program at the University of Michigan.*

CYNTHIA J. FINELLI *is managing director of the Center for Research on Learning and Teaching (CRLT) North, a joint venture between the University of Michigan College of Engineering and CRLT. She is also an associate research scientist of engineering education.*

**9**

*This chapter investigates the barriers faced by singers of all racial backgrounds when performing spirituals and African American art songs and suggests ways to eliminate those barriers.*

# Singing Down the Barriers: Encouraging Singers of All Racial Backgrounds to Perform Music by African American Composers

*Caroline Helton, Emery Stephens*

The idea for our project developed in a doctoral seminar taught by Caroline Helton, a white faculty member in voice at the University of Michigan. In a presentation on the performance practice of singing spirituals, Emery Stephens, an African American graduate student in the seminar, concluded by encouraging everyone in the room (all white with the exception of one Asian student) to program spirituals on their recitals. The halting reply was "We can't because we're not black," to which Emery replied, "Why not?" Thus began our journey toward investigating the barriers singers face when they attempt to perform spirituals and art songs by African American composers. However, finding out about the barriers is useless unless we can break them down and allow all students to benefit musically, artistically, and socially from the experience of singing this repertoire.

As we began to explore this subject, four questions emerged to guide our research:

• What are the barriers that singers from all racial backgrounds face when performing art songs and spirituals by African American composers?
• How do students and teachers confront their preconceptions when learning any piece of music (for example, a female student singing a song from

NEW DIRECTIONS FOR TEACHING AND LEARNING, no. 111, Fall 2007 © Wiley Periodicals, Inc.
Published online in Wiley InterScience (www.interscience.wiley.com) • DOI: 10.1002/tl.288

a man's perspective)? Specifically, how can that process be applied to learning spirituals and art songs by African Americans?

- How is a singer's outlook on racial dynamics affected by studying and performing these pieces?
- What do we need to do as educators to enable singers from all racial backgrounds to become more comfortable performing this repertoire?

Before we turn to these questions, we would like to define some of the musical terms we are using and give a brief historical overview of the issues that make performance of this repertoire a complicated matter.

The term *art song* refers to a composition for voice and piano in which the composer has chosen to set to music a preexisting text (*poetry* as opposed to *lyrics*), as Franz Schubert did with the Goethe poem "Erlkönig" and Aaron Copeland did with some of Emily Dickinson's works. The resulting composition involves a musical union in which piano and vocal lines support and complement one another in a way that elucidates the composer's conception of the poem. Unlike folk songs, which are anonymous and passed down through an oral tradition, art songs remain the domain of the "trained" composer, who is intending the pieces to be performed by classical musicians. However, this distinction is not always complete, because trained composers have often been drawn to set existing folk melodies to a similarly intentioned accompaniment. Even though these settings are of folk melodies, they more resemble art songs because they are written with the skills of the trained singer and pianist in mind. African American spirituals fall into this category of "folk song settings," as they are drawn from the largest body of folk songs in America, popular with white and black audiences alike for over a century, whether they are sung solo or in choral arrangements.

Our modern cultural quandary concerning performance practice stems from the complex history surrounding the provenance of spirituals. Early African American spirituals, once called "Negro spirituals" or "plantation slave songs," were inspired by African and Western European musical and religious traditions and were originally sung in "slave dialect." These songs were adopted and sung by slaves as work songs during their daily activities. These pieces are thus intimately connected to the history of slavery in the United States (Southern, 1971).

The nineteenth century also saw the meteoric rise in the popularity of minstrel shows, in which white performers blackened their faces and played stock characters modeled on slave stereotypes. Beginning in the 1840s and for several decades thereafter, minstrel shows were the most popular stage entertainment in America. Black performers were eventually allowed to take part in minstrel shows, also wearing black face makeup. Ironically, this was one of the first professional outlets for black singers, who were by and large prohibited from performing for a wider audience in any other genre (Hamm, 1979; Southern, 1971).

NEW DIRECTIONS FOR TEACHING AND LEARNING • DOI: 10.1002/tl

The current sensitivity to race in the performance of art songs and spirituals by African American composers stems from our nation's history of slavery and oppression on the one hand and the legacy of minstrelsy and its stereotyping and mocking of African Americans on the other. Though these events are now far removed from our experience, their repercussions are still palpable in our cultural dynamics today. Time has not healed this wound but rather obscured the path to the cure. Since art songs and spirituals by African Americans connect directly to both of these historical phenomena, performing them could provide a means of exploring and defusing the racial sensitivity we feel today (Plant, 2005).

Our inquiry began as a discussion of the barriers experienced by singers of all races when approaching this repertoire. To find out more about how singers of today view this delicate topic, we developed an e-mail survey that we sent to five hundred singers in the professional world and at academic institutions. We received 218 responses, a response rate of 43 percent. The survey included questions on demographics (gender, age, ethnic background, religious affiliation), musical training, exposure to art songs and spirituals by African Americans, preferences of vocal performance style, and attitudes toward performance of this repertoire by singers of all racial backgrounds (focusing on perceptions of authenticity). Approximately one-quarter (23 percent) of the respondents were African American and three quarters (73 percent) Caucasian. Nearly three-quarters (72 percent) of the respondents have at least one degree in music, 50 percent identified themselves as voice teachers and professional singers, and 39 percent described themselves as voice students. Sixty-two percent said they had never received any instruction on singing African American art songs or spirituals in their private or institutional voice studio, but an overwhelming majority (87 percent) said they would like to perform this literature.

Our analysis of the responses to the question about challenges to performing this repertoire broke down into four categories. Roughly one-quarter of responses expressed fears of inauthenticity or needing permission to perform the repertoire. Another quarter cited lack of availability or knowledge of where to find pieces. A slightly greater number of respondents felt that they lacked sufficient stylistic knowledge or guidance to interpret the repertoire correctly and respectfully, and a small number of singers cited ignorance (on the part of the general public or colleagues or their own musical shortcomings) as a barrier.

The survey also asked about the extent to which a performer's race contributes to the authenticity of his or her performance of this repertoire. Approximately 25 percent of the respondents felt that race greatly contributed to perceptions of authenticity, while 62 percent rated the contribution moderate, and 13 percent felt that the race of the performer did not play any role at all. When asked to explain their rating, responses indicating that race played a major role came from African Americans, who felt a strong sense of ownership of the repertoire, and non–African Americans, who assumed that they wouldn't be accepted by audiences:

> I think that at this point race plays a major part in the authenticity of singing African American art songs, simply because many teachers of other races have not taken the time to know this material well enough to teach students how to approach them with understanding and appreciation for the history and culture behind them.

> I think African Americans can sing these types of songs more authentically, and I feel like I don't have as much of a right to perform this type of music because I'm not black. But I think if more singers of all races were to sing this type of material, it would become more widely accepted.

The majority of respondents, however, felt that singers of all racial backgrounds must actively work to connect to the literature they sing. They said that it may be easier for some African American singers who have had certain experiences to connect to the repertoire, but that does not rule out the responsibility borne by any singer to create an authentic and committed performance; in other words, race alone does not bestow authenticity on the singer. Respondents observed, "It's not so much race as it is level of familiarity with the style" and "A good understanding of the history of African American art songs, the text of the song, and how to properly sing it is necessary, and these factors have nothing to do with race."

In fact, when asked how comfortable they would be if singers of all races performed this repertoire, virtually all of respondents (99 percent) reported a high or moderate level of comfort. In response to open-ended questions, two singers spoke eloquently of the possibility for cross-cultural communication:

> As a fellow African American, it is my duty, and the duty of other African Americans, to continue performing the songs of our past to others. I believe that is very important to do; however, when people of other races sing these wonderful songs the message of continuing the story is extended to a greater family of people, beyond race.

> I do not believe that music has a soul, but it does leave the imprints of peoples' spirits and communicates on a deeper level than our verbal language can ever begin to communicate.

It is this very idea that leads us to explore ways of helping artists from all backgrounds perform this music.

Our first step was to analyze how artists confront their preconceptions when learning a song that requires portraying a very different character from the performer's own identity. For singers, the artistic process involves internalizing the multifaceted layers of meaning in a text (often in a foreign language) and expressing that interpretation through music, with beautiful vocalism, artistry, and dramatic commitment—no small task. In the world of opera, there is also a need for performers to appear believable in their roles, and directors often cast accordingly. It is true that in opera there is a history of stretching this verisimilitude because of vocal ideals rather than physical ones (pants roles, older women singing the part of young girls), but as a general rule audience members' expectations are not confused by what they see on stage in opera.

Art song, by contrast, is completely different. Each song presents its own unique world for the performer to inhabit. It would be a boring recital indeed if the singer chose only music that represented his or her physical appearance. We are called on to sing in many different languages, from the perspective of opposite genders and cultures far removed from our own. To make each situation believable for the audience, we must be guided by the composer's musical interpretation of the text to create a dramatically committed and coherent performance. Given that singers do this on a regular basis, why should we hesitate to sing from the perspective of another's race? The answer to that question is of course bound up in our culture's history of racism and oppression, but we would like to propose that the accepted performance practice of art songs offers a real opportunity to heal some of those wounds.

In the survey many African American singers said (to paraphrase), "If I can sing from a nineteenth-century white German man's point of view, why can't a white person sing from a slave's point of view?" At the University of Michigan School of Music, Theatre, and Dance, we invited a small but diverse group of undergraduate students to do just that. Our group consisted of two white female singers, two white male singers, and one black male singer, who first answered a series of questions about their backgrounds and their opinions of and previous exposure to art songs and spirituals by African Americans. With the help of their studio teachers as well as a course regularly offered at our university on the song literature of African Americans, the students explored their chosen repertoire. Some of them had guidance from African American professors, and some did not. At the end of the term, we conducted focus groups with the students, asking them specific questions about their expectations, their artistic process, and their discoveries. When they spoke of their experiences singing these spirituals and art songs by African American composers, many of them remarked on the freedom they felt because they had finally been given permission to sing from this perspective:

> I was glad to have the opportunity to perform this repertoire *with permission,* because I've only ever seen black singers perform it and I've always wanted to be able to.

> Some of my pieces you couldn't tell what the perspective was, but some you could. I learned to dive in with confidence and push hesitation out of the way because we take on different characters all the time.

> The main idea is to get ideas or emotion across no matter what your race.

The question of how their outlook on racial dynamics was affected can begin to be answered by looking at some of the other comments from our focus group in which students talked of the insights they gained after learning and performing these pieces:

> "Singing outside the box" breaks cultural barriers and makes it much easier to connect to others. Performing makes you learn way more than just reading about it; it makes the experience much stronger.

> Everybody learns about the Harlem Renaissance, but doing it [performing songs by poets and composers from that era] was way more powerful.

> You need to understand the struggle and some of African American history and know how each song relates to the struggle. Each story is told from a different perspective.

> I gained the most insight when I did my first mock performance—after the music was learned and memorized—and I was making choices about how I was going to make people believe me. I thought that, since I'm African American, my connection would be automatic, but my insight came through real performance.

All these singers were struck by the strong emotional content of the pieces and the music's unique ability to convey the universality of experience. One singer astutely summed up the potential of this musical tool for social awareness: "As a soloist, you search for the music that *you* are; the experience [is] more lasting, a self-fulfillment. [You have to engage in] more self-exploration because you're the sole communicator." In other words, you are required to *empathize*, not just sympathize, to do your job as a performer, and in art songs, you don't have costume, lights, or makeup to help you convince the audience.

What do we need to do as educators to enable singers from all racial backgrounds to become more comfortable performing this repertoire? First of all, voice teachers of all races should work together to convey the message that all students have "permission" to perform this repertoire. Second, to guide students toward committed, informed performances, we need to familiarize ourselves with the body of song literature and its proper performance practice (see Dunn-Powell, 2005; Steinhaus-Jordan, 2005; and Plant, 2005, for repertoire resources as well as discussion of performance practice). Third, we need to assign these pieces to students as part of their regular diet of quality music that is good for their voices and their development as artists. Fourth, we can program these songs in our own recitals so that our students can experience a live example of how it's done. Finally, we should follow up by talking to students about their experiences of singing these songs, which is easy to do in one-on-one studio teaching.

We plan to expand this study by continuing to collect and analyze stories about the barriers to and the impact of performing music by African American composers. As part of this work we have begun visiting colleges and universities around the country to present a lecture-recital and master class that would enable students who have learned pieces to perform them and to reflect with us on the impact the experience has on them as performers and audience members. Initial reactions at both campuses and academic conferences have been overwhelmingly positive from faculty and students of all racial backgrounds.

Performing the recital repertoire of art songs and spirituals by African Americans can be a wonderfully useful way for singers to confront their own preconceptions around race and performance practice, important issues for future professionals who will be performing for an increasingly diverse audience. There is no better place to attempt this task than in our colleges and universities, where teachers can guide and students can explore, pushing beyond the boundaries of their cultural assumptions in a safe environment where discussion of difficult topics is part of the process of their education as artists and citizens of the world.

## References

Dunn-Powell, R. "The African-American Spiritual: Preparation and Performance Considerations." *NATS Journal of Singing*, 2005, *61*(5), 469–475.

Hamm, C. *Yesterdays: Popular Song in America.* New York: Norton, 1979.

Plant, L. "Singing African-American Spirituals: A Reflection on Racial Barriers in Classical Vocal Music." *NATS Journal of Singing*, 2005, *61*(5), 451–468.

Southern, E. *The Music of Black Americans: A History.* New York: Norton, 1971.

Steinhaus-Jordan, B. "Black Spiritual Art Song: Interpretive Guidelines for Studio Teachers." *NATS Journal of Singing*, 2005, *61*(5), 477–485.

CAROLINE HELTON *is clinical assistant professor of music (voice) at the University of Michigan School of Music, Theatre, and Dance.*

EMERY STEPHENS *is a doctoral student in vocal performance at the University of Michigan School of Music, Theatre, and Dance.*

NEW DIRECTIONS FOR TEACHING AND LEARNING • DOI: 10.1002/tl

**10**

*This chapter offers an example of a discipline-specific approach to diversity education and its impact on student learning.*

# Diversity Education and Identity Development in an Information Technology Course

*Eileen M. Trauth, R. Neill Johnson, Allison Morgan, Haiyan Huang, Jeria Quesenberry*

One of the major challenges facing today's information technology sector is the diversity of the labor force. Globalization is having a significant influence on the information technology (IT) industry (Walsham, 2000) through offshore outsourcing (Carmel and Agarwal, 2002), global software development (Sahay, Nicholson, and Krishna, 2003), and global information systems management. These new kinds of work, requiring cross-cultural collaboration, demand new sets of knowledge and skills. As opportunities for global expansion and outsourcing increase, so does the demand for greater diversity in the domestic workforce. Recruiting and retaining "the best and the brightest" in the IT field demands that the profession welcome all individuals regardless of gender, race, nationality, or other identity characteristics (Trauth, Huang, Quesenberry, and Morgan, 2007).

A particular educational challenge for universities that are not located in major metropolitan areas rich in demographic diversity is how to prepare those in the future labor force to value diversity and understand the ways in which their behaviors can contribute to or detract from a welcoming climate. In response to this need, Eileen Trauth designed a course titled Human Diversity in the Global Information Economy in spring 2005

NEW DIRECTIONS FOR TEACHING AND LEARNING, no. 111, Fall 2007   © Wiley Periodicals, Inc.
Published online in Wiley InterScience (www.interscience.wiley.com) • DOI: 10.1002/tl.289

when she was a fellow of the Multicultural Teaching Academy, a project sponsored by the Schreyer Institute for Teaching Excellence and the Africana Research Center at Penn State. In this course, first taught in fall 2005, students examined the effects of human diversity on the analysis, development, and use of information systems and technology. They also reflected on their own identities and drew on their experiences of "privilege" and "otherness" to develop solutions to problems faced by workers and clients in IT settings.

## Building Diversity into an Information Technology Course

Building on an analytical framework developed for diversity and IT research (Trauth and others, 2006) and an existing framework for culturally inclusive teaching (Wlodkowski and Ginsberg, 1995), the authors created a diversity-focused career preparation course. Through readings, discussions, and team-based case scenarios, students in the course explored multiple diversity issues—including gender, race, sexual orientation, socioeconomic class, and age. Examples of the curricular focus include the following:

- *Gender.* Women are significantly underrepresented in the IT workforce everywhere in the world (Arnold and Niederman, 2001; Camp, 1997). Students discussed gender and Internet behavior, technology and gender stereotypes, and sexual harassment in the workplace.
- *Race.* African Americans, Hispanics, and Native Americans are also underrepresented in the sciences and technology disciplines (BEST, 2004). In-class learning activities asked students to consider the connection between race and technology adoption and how to manage issues that could be present in multiracial project teams. In addition, students participated in an out-of-class, peer-led discussion facilitated by the Race Relations Project at Penn State.
- *Sexual orientation.* Many of our students come from isolated rural communities where sexual minorities are invisible and therefore unknown. This was the first course many of these students had had that addressed sexual orientation.
- *Socioeconomic status.* This topic was explored in terms of the "digital divide," the gap between those who have the resources to participate with information technology and those who do not.
- *Cross-cultural diversity.* In a semester-long assignment, students corresponded electronically with students in one of seven different countries to design a Web-based information tool for users in that country. In their project reports and presentations, students were asked to discuss the sociocultural context of their assigned country, provide the results of their

cross-cultural analysis, and reflect on their cross-cultural virtual work experiences.

## Parameters of Course Research

Thematic analysis of two individual reflection papers provides the basis for our discussion of learning gains attained by students who took Human Diversity in the Global Information Economy in fall 2005. In the first assignment, completed in the fourth week of the fourteen-week course, students reflected on their educational and life experiences related to diversity, including their participation in the out-of-class peer-facilitated Race Relations Project. This assignment provided a "baseline account" of each student's thoughts on diversity as well as reflections on the first few weeks of the course. In the second assignment, completed in week 13, students applied what they had learned to determine how best to meet the IT needs of clients and colleagues with identities different from their own. The decision to include this sensitivity to "the other" came from Trauth's prior research into cross-cultural issues (Trauth, 2000) and on gender in the information technology field (Trauth, 2002).

We looked at both assignments for evidence that students had attained three desired learning outcomes: critical analysis of the link between increased productivity and a diverse IT workforce, evaluation of self as an agent or target of discrimination within the larger framework of institutionalized privileges and oppressions, and ability to identify the challenges and needs of diverse IT clients and coworkers in specific cross-cultural contexts. The third outcome was more explicit in the final individual reflection paper. Since most students in the course were white, we applied Helms's U.S. white racial identity development model (1990) in analyzing students' reflections. The Helms model has six stages. The first three (Contact, Disintegration, Reintegration) involve the white subject's attempts to confront and move beyond his or her own racism. Helms links these stages together as Phase 1: Abandonment of Racism. The last three stages (Pseudo-Independent, Immersion/Emersion, Autonomy) Helms labels Phase 2: Defining a Nonracist White Identity. We did not present this model to students in the course; nevertheless, we found the model useful in interpreting students' attainment of the second and third learning outcomes.

Of the thirty-seven students enrolled in the course, twenty-three participated in our research. We defined as the "majority" twelve traditional-age, straight, white males and as the "minority" eleven students consisting of five straight, white females (four of traditional age and one returning adult); three traditional-age, straight, Asian American females; one traditional-age, straight, Asian American male; one traditional-age, white, gay man; and one traditional-age, white lesbian. In our analysis we compared the learning gains of majority and minority students.

## Analysis of Student Learning Outcomes

All minority students and over 80 percent of the majority students attained outcome 1, critical analysis of the link between increased productivity and a diverse information technology workforce. Most students noted that the course had expanded their definition of diversity beyond race and gender to include such things as socioeconomic status, age, ability, sexual orientation, and religion. Most also responded positively to the evidence presented in course readings and in class sessions connecting creativity and business success to diversity broadly defined. Several students provided well-argued critiques of particular articles and guest lecturers, but they found the evidence persuasive on the whole. Only two majority students rejected the evidence entirely. Although their arguments were not well researched, we were pleased that these two men were able to express their dissent.

Far more typical was the reflection of a minority student who contrasted this course to humanities courses that "dealt with race in very emotional ways" and concluded, "Although I've learned a great deal about people who are different from me in those classes, I was very happy to finally see diversity dealt with in an unemotional, academic fashion in this class. I am not particularly interested in blame games—I just want solutions to social inequalities." Thus a discipline-specific research context seems to have been equally important to majority and minority students.

All students made some progress toward the more challenging outcomes 2 and 3: self-evaluation as agent or target of discrimination and ability to identify information technology challenges and needs of an "other."

The four majority students who showed the most significant learning gains on outcome 2 were able to observe their own identity conflicts and growth in terms we can recognize through Helms's stages of white racial identity development. For example, one student writes, "I thought that after three years in college I had a broad outlook on life and I was open to diversity. After the race relations course [to] which I was assigned, I realized that I am back in my bubble and have surrounded myself with people of similar backgrounds as myself." He goes on to talk about how his fraternity discriminates on a number of fronts and how he intends to change that as an older member. Students like these are clearly aware of their white privilege as a result of their experiences in the course.

For four of the eleven minority students, the outcome 2 learning gains are expressed in terms of a new understanding of and empathy for those with a majority perspective attained through critical analysis of their own cultural advantages. Contrary to our expectations, the minority students who had considered themselves most culturally advantaged (they had the most exposure living or interacting in diverse communities) at the start of the course were those who showed the most significant learning gains with respect to analysis of self as agent or target of discrimination. Typical of this subgroup is the reflection of the white lesbian student: "One of the most insightful experiences for me in this class was finally talking about diversity with people who weren't already diversity-trained. Just as I have almost always talked about gay issues with only gay people, I have spent hours discussing race relations among people of all races—except other white people. Class discussions and the Race Relations Project were large eye-opening experiences for me to learn what my fellow students believe." One of the things that her majority classmates taught her is that the digital divide affects people in rural areas, too—that access to technology is not only a concern for poor urban people but also for rural people of widely varying economic means. They also helped her avoid putting a "race" label on issues that are really about socioeconomic status.

For the final individual reflection paper, ten of the eleven minority students and ten of the twelve majority students creatively outlined the needs of information technology workers and users who have multiple identities very different from their own (outcome 3). Although their solutions were not always the most equitable, these students genuinely tried to put themselves into others' shoes as they imagined difficulties their characters would encounter on the job as well as needs they would have as IT clients. Each of the three exceptions created a worker or client who was a thinly disguised image of that person or a close relative. These are safe subjects for analysis, but they do not encourage creative problem solving outside one's own cultural or socioeconomic comfort zone.

## Lessons Learned and Implications for Future Research and Teaching

The one consistent finding across all participants in the study is that students were more receptive to diversity education when it was presented in the context of the discipline. We also discovered that it is possible for students to make progress in their racial identity development over the course of one semester. Tatum (1992) states that it is not only possible but even "common to witness beginning transformations in classes with race-related content" (p. 18). In our study, one third of the students reported what we consider a remarkable transformation. The reflective papers of one third of our "culturally disadvantaged" majority students provide evidence that the course was for them a catalyst for substantial self-realization. In addition, we were surprised that about the same proportion of minority students (arguably those most culturally advantaged at the beginning of the course) reported significant learning gains in understanding the majority perspective and developing empathy for their majority peers.

Future research should investigate whether identity models for non-white and other minority populations (black racial identity development models, sexual minority identity development models, and so on) are helpful in assessing the learning of minority students in such career development courses. The present research sample had only one population large enough to apply a particular identity development model. However, we believe that students tend to focus only on the identity that is most salient for them at the moment. For example, the salient issue for the four traditional-age, straight, white women in this study was gender, *not* race. These women made few gains in terms of white racial identity development, perhaps because they were focused on their minority status as women in a male-dominated discipline. However, studies with a larger number of participants would reveal whether such women's learning gains would be comparable in kind and proportion to those of their male counterparts.

Finally, faculty who develop courses such as Human Diversity in the Global Information Economy would be well advised to design learning activities that challenge students to examine their own identity in terms of power and privilege as a necessary correlate to doing research on the relationship between diversity, creativity and inventiveness, and success.

## References

Arnold, D., and Niederman, F. "The Global Workforce." *Communications of the ACM,* 2001, *44*(7), 31–33.

BEST: Building Engineering and Science Talent. *A Bridge for All: Higher Education Design Principles to Broaden Participation in Science, Technology, Engineering, and Mathematics.* San Diego, Calif.: BEST, 2004. http://www.bestworkforce.org. Accessed on May 30, 2007.

Camp, T. "The Incredible Shrinking Pipeline." *Communications of the ACM,* 1997, *40*(10), 103–110.

Carmel, E., and Agarwal, R. "The Maturation of Offshore Sourcing of Information Technology Work." *MIS Quarterly Executive,* 2002, *1*(2), 65–77.

Helms, J. E. "Toward a Model of White Racial Identity Development." *Black and White Racial Identity: Theory, Research, and Practice.* Contributions in Afro-American and African Studies, no. 129. Westport, Conn.: Greenwood Press, 1990.

Sahay, S., Nicholson, B., and Krishna, S. *Global IT Outsourcing: Software Development Across Borders.* Cambridge: Cambridge University Press, 2003.

Tatum, B. D. "Talking About Race, Learning About Racism: The Application of Racial Identity Development Theory in the Classroom." *Harvard Educational Review,* 1992, *62*(1), 1–24.

Trauth, E. M. *The Culture of an Information Economy: Influences and Impacts in the Republic of Ireland.* Dordrecht, Netherlands: Kluwer Academic, 2000.

Trauth, E. M. "Odd Girl Out: An Individual Differences Perspective on Women in the IT Profession." *Information Technology and People,* 2002, *15*(2), 98–118 (special issue).

Trauth, E. M., Huang, H., Quesenberry, J., and Morgan, A. "Leveraging Diversity in Information Systems and Technology Education in the Global Workplace." In G. R. Lowry and R. L. Turner (eds.), *Information Systems and Technology Education: From the University to the Workplace.* Hershey, Pa.: Information Science Reference, 2007.

Trauth, E. M., and others. "Investigating the Existence and Value of Diversity in the Global IT Workforce: An Analytical Framework." In F. Niederman and T. Ferratt (eds.), *Managing Information Technology Human Resources.* Greenwich, Conn.: Information Age, 2006.

Walsham, G. "IT, Globalization and Cultural Diversity." In C. Avgerou and G. Walsham (eds.), *Information Technology in Context: Studies from the Perspective of Developing Countries.* Aldershot, England: Ashgate, 2000.

Wlodkowski, R. J., and Ginsberg, M. B. *Diversity and Motivation: Culturally Responsive Teaching.* San Francisco: Jossey-Bass, 1995.

EILEEN M. TRAUTH *is a professor of information sciences and technology and director of the Center for the Information Society at the Pennsylvania State University.*

R. NEILL JOHNSON *is a research associate of the Schreyer Institute for Teaching Excellence at the Pennsylvania State University.*

ALLISON MORGAN, HAIYAN HUANG, *and* JERIA QUESENBERRY *are Ph.D. candidates and teaching fellows in the College of Information Sciences and Technology at the Pennsylvania State University.*

NEW DIRECTIONS FOR TEACHING AND LEARNING • DOI: 10.1002/tl

# 11

*This chapter discusses the benefits and constraints of a simulation-based strategy for enhancing civic competence among introductory government students, an approach that shows promise for closing racial and gender gaps in political efficacy and participation.*

# Simulations and the Dynamics of Racial and Gender Gaps in Civic Competence

Jeffrey L. Bernstein

This chapter takes the somewhat unorthodox stance that the central purpose of an introductory political science course is not to prepare students for future political science courses but rather to prepare them for a lifetime of democratic citizenship. It suggests that the way to do this is not by primarily teaching content but by offering opportunities to learn and practice citizenship skills. After detailing the course I designed to teach these skills, I present evidence that suggests that this approach may address some long-term inequalities in political participation and engagement across racial and gender lines.

## Citizenship Training in Political Science Courses

Discussions of the role citizenship training should play in education are as old as the discipline of political science (see Bennett, 1999; and Dewey, [1927] 1954). In some ways these discussions reflect issues raised by Larry Cuban (1999) in *How Scholars Trumped Teachers*. Cuban discusses how the dominant paradigm of higher education has shifted over time from valuing the teaching of students to valuing service to society to the current state of affairs, where scholarship has trumped teaching and service. As a result of this shift, academics have understandably come to identify themselves

NEW DIRECTIONS FOR TEACHING AND LEARNING, no. 111, Fall 2007 © Wiley Periodicals, Inc.
Published online in Wiley InterScience (www.interscience.wiley.com) • DOI: 10.1002/tl.290

more with their disciplines and less with their roles as teachers and their responsibility to serve society.

The introductory American government class reflects these tensions. My own research on my own teaching practices and those of six colleagues at my institution reveals a remarkable diversity of goals, pedagogical methods, and assessment strategies at use in this course. These differences are not trivial, as each would lead to dramatically different strategies for teaching the class.

The context in which I teach this course has led me to move away from the content-driven model and toward the citizenship model. Political Science 112: American Government, at Eastern Michigan University, is an introductory-level course that has traditionally been a required course in the general education program. The students are diverse in terms of demographic makeup. During the 2005–06 academic year my students were 56 percent female and 33 percent African American; 3 percent were Asian American, and one student was Latina. Students also vary in their ability, motivation, and preparation. Because the course is required for all students at the university, it is rare for more than 5 percent of the students to have an interest in taking future political science courses. Most take the class reluctantly, suffer through it, and emerge unaffected. While the situation may be less bleak at schools where students have a choice whether or not to take this class, few students would find that this kind of course has life-changing potential.

As a political scientist committed to helping students understand that they can make a difference politically and to helping them find their political voice, I find this status quo unsatisfactory, particularly from a multicultural teaching perspective. The literature on political knowledge and participation reveals large gaps across race and gender. Women and African Americans show lower levels of political knowledge when measured by answering questions such as "Who is the speaker of the House of Representatives?" (Davis and Silver, 2003; Delli Carpini and Keeter, 1991; 1996). Although the political science literature suggests that informed political decisions can be made even with limited factual knowledge (Downs, 1957; Lupia and McCubbins, 1998; Popkin, 1991; Zaller, 1992), this perceived lack of knowledge can often be an impediment to participation, particularly among women (Delli Carpini and Keeter, 1996; Rapoport, 1981; Verba, Burns, and Schlozman, 1997).

Racial and gender gaps appear not only in political knowledge but also in most forms of political participation (Rosenstone and Hansen, 1993; Teixeira, 1992; Verba, Burns, and Schlozman, 1997). As with political knowledge, these gaps are not *caused* by race or gender but rather reflect other intervening factors, such as people's differences in both internal political efficacy (their belief that they can understand the political system) and external political efficacy (their belief that they can affect the political system). These gaps may also reflect the differences in financial and informational resources that condition political participation. Although there is little a government class can do to address the financial gaps that map onto race and gender, it seems quite reasonable that it can close gaps in informational resources and in both types of political efficacy. The impact of education looms large; it can be, in the words of the social progressive Horace Mann (1957, p. 87), "the great equalizer" in society.

## A Skills-Based Approach to Citizenship Education

In light of all this, my teaching goals for the class have changed since I exited graduate school. I now pay less attention to "covering" a wide range of course content; instead, I choose to focus in depth on what I believe to be the critical aspects of the course, aiming to "uncover" these areas (Wiggins and McTighe, 1998; see Calder, 2006, for an elaboration of this theme in the context of a history survey course). I'm not convinced that providing more information will enhance the citizenship-oriented goals I have adopted, nor am I convinced that it will address the significant and pressing gender and racial gaps we see in society. On the contrary, focusing on something more meaningful and more applied will maximize the chance that this course will have an impact on students when they complete it.

I choose to center my citizenship focus on giving students the opportunity to learn the skills they need to be effective citizens. Effective citizenship resides in the head (knowledge), the heart (commitment), and the hand (action). In my course, I address the knowledge aspect through course content, somewhat deemphasized but certainly not ignored. I address the commitment aspect by modeling my own civic engagement and by offering students numerous examples of others who have shown similar commitment (the vignettes in Frantzich, 2005, are particularly instructive). Action, however, is where the bulk of my time is spent, giving students practice in building political skills. I focus on three citizenship skills:

- Skill in managing information—teaching students how to make sense of an overwhelming volume of political information, managing contradictions between sources, and assessing the credibility and usefulness of different sources
- Skill in managing people—working effectively with others to help attain one's political goals and working in civil opposition to others who oppose one's goals
- Skill in managing rules—understanding that rules often determine outcomes and that one must learn how to use the given rules to one's advantage (and, when appropriate, to modify the rules to make them work to one's advantage)

Beyond this, what is most important is instilling in my students the belief that they are sufficiently skilled to be effective political actors. If they did not believe this, all would be for naught; even highly skilled actors who don't believe they can do it *won't* do it.

My vehicle for achieving these goals is a series of simulations. Four times during the semester, the class takes a one-week break from the regular routine and engages in simulations. The hundred-student class divides into four groups, each of which engages in a legislative-style simulation around a hot political issue. The students in this study rotated among simulations on affirmative action, eminent domain, school prayer, and the war on terrorism. One week before the simulation begins, the students receive a packet of eight to ten short readings on the issue, drawn from a variety of sources (news articles, opinion pieces, blogs, press releases, and other documents). They are asked to write a three-page paper that uses the articles to articulate a position on the issue. Since they do this four times during the semester, they get practice in managing information, the first of my three target skills.

Following this, the class engages in a simulation based on the issue. A "status quo" of current policy is presented to the students, who then propose amendments to the status quo and attempt to build support for their proposed amendments. For example, one line from the status quo used in the war on terrorism simulation reads, "Though the United States will consult the United Nations before waging war (unless the situation requires a quick, surprise attack), the United States is in no way bound by the decisions of the United Nations." Students often focus on this line and write proposals that might suggest that the United States must be bound by the decisions of the UN (or more rarely, that the United States has no obligation even to consult with the UN on issues of national security). The students spend the first day of the simulation meeting classmates, exchanging views (often using a think-pair-share-square exercise), and starting to draft proposals. Day 2 is spent finalizing proposals and building support in anticipation of voting on proposals on the third day; all the while, students are gaining skills in working with allies and in civil opposition to opponents, the second target skill.

The third and final day of the simulation is spent voting on proposals that aim to change the current policy; any proposals that get approved would then change the current government policies on the issue. In each simulation, a five-member rules committee determines which proposals can be considered and in what order. In some cases the rules committee is elected by the class, while in others its members are appointed by the facilitator. Sometimes we require a simple majority to pass a proposal; in other simulations we require a two-thirds majority. Finally, we sometimes vote by secret ballot and at other times by a show of hands. By changing the rules from simulation to simulation, students gain practice working under the constraints imposed by the rules; they also learn through experience that rules truly do help determine outcomes, the third target skill.

## Some Evidence for the Effectiveness of This Approach

The results presented here are based on a survey given at the beginning and end of the term. The survey inquired about political interest and beliefs, perceived skill levels, and levels of political activity. To facilitate comparisons across the pretest and posttest data, only students who completed both tests are included in the results. This slightly biases the findings in an upward direction, as the poorest students (those who did not complete the class) are excluded from the analysis.

**Gains in Political Skills.** Table 11.1 reports on skill gains across racial and gender categories. Questions about skills were divided into informational items (for example, "I can understand the pros and cons of political arguments"), interpersonal items ("I can deal with conflict when it comes up"), and a single strategy item ("I can develop strategies for political action"); all items were scored from 1 (lowest evaluation of one's skills) to 6 (highest self-evaluation). Table 11.1 reveals that students showed dramatic gains across all items. The strategy item showed particularly large gains from low pretest scores.

**Gains in Political Interest and Efficacy.** While gains in perceived skills are important, from a multicultural perspective the ultimate aim is to demonstrate an impact in political interest and participation and in political efficacy. If female and African American students show gains in these areas, they may emerge as effective political actors, reversing the gender and racial gaps cited earlier. Table 11.2 presents results for both areas. For political participation, I use pretest and posttest measures of whether students follow politics regularly—it is unrealistic to expect any greater behavioral changes to take place during one semester. The first two columns of the table demonstrate small gains in following politics. African American males, who had started out as the group claiming to follow politics the most

### Table 11.1. Skills Gains Stratified by Race and Gender

|  | Pretest Skill Levels (0–6 scale) | | | Posttest Skill Levels (0–6 scale) | | |
|---|---|---|---|---|---|---|
|  | Information | People | Strategy | Information | People | Strategy |
| White males (n = 37) | 3.57 | 3.82 | 2.78 | 4.50 | 4.37 | 4.00 |
| White females (n = 54) | 3.44 | 3.84 | 2.41 | 4.59 | 4.45 | 3.72 |
| African American males (n = 20) | 3.55 | 4.37 | 2.95 | 4.67 | 4.70 | 4.05 |
| African American females (n = 18) | 3.22 | 3.72 | 2.72 | 3.76 | 4.08 | 3.29 |
| All students (N = 129) | 3.46 | 3.90 | 2.64 | 4.43 | 4.42 | 3.80 |

NEW DIRECTIONS FOR TEACHING AND LEARNING • DOI: 10.1002/tl

### Table 11.2  Gains in Following Politics and in Political Efficacy, Stratified by Race and Gender

|  | Follow Politics Regularly (0–6) | | Feel Qualified to Participate (0–6) | | Feel I Can Make a Difference (0–6) | |
|---|---|---|---|---|---|---|
|  | Pretest | Posttest | Pretest | Posttest | Pretest | Posttest |
| White males (n = 37) | 3.11 | 3.57 | 3.19 | 4.27 | 3.14 | 4.30 |
| White females (n = 54) | 3.08 | 3.53 | 3.09 | 3.98 | 3.61 | 4.37 |
| African American males (n = 20) | 3.56 | 3.72 | 3.45 | 4.10 | 3.90 | 4.50 |
| African American females (n = 18) | 3.27 | 3.00 | 2.67 | 2.82 | 3.50 | 3.29 |
| All students (N = 129) | 3.18 | 3.50 | 3.12 | 3.93 | 3.50 | 4.23 |

closely, experience particularly modest gains but still emerge in the leading position at the end of the course. African American females actually experienced a decline in how much they followed politics; I will discuss this result shortly.

The middle columns of the table report dramatic gains in students' feelings that they were qualified to participate in politics. The average gain of 0.81 points on a 6-point scale is quite significant; substantively, it indicates that the activities being practiced in class help students achieve at least one of the most important aims of the class. Finally, dramatic gains were also seen on a question asking students if they believed they could make a difference in the political system. For both of these results, however, African American women once again lagged behind the other students.

## Discussion

Based on these results and on others reported at greater length elsewhere (Bernstein, forthcoming), I conclude that my approach is successful in helping most students gain confidence in their civic skills and as a result emerge more efficacious regarding their ability to understand politics and to make a difference. For white males, white females, and African American males, the simulations resulted in dramatic gains in political skills, which translated into gains in political interest and efficacy. Considering that much of the gap in adult political participation for white women and African American men results from an efficacy gap, these findings are encouraging, for they suggest the possibility that these students may be more ready to pick up the mantle of political activism as they mature and leave college.

The findings for African American women are troubling, to say the least. These students experience the smallest gains in skills and in feeling qualified to participate in politics. They also *decline* in how closely they follow politics and in feeling they can make a difference in politics. On average, these findings are explainable. African American women in the class began class far less knowledgeable about politics than their classmates (they answered an average of 3.83 factual questions out of 10 correctly on the pretest, compared to 5.56 correct answers for the rest of the class) and feeling less qualified to participate in politics (see Table 11.2, middle columns). As a group, they performed much worse in the simulations (their simulation participation grades averaged 2.06 on a 5-point scale, compared to 3.14 for the other students). This was partly a result of their attendance (in the last two simulations, the only ones for which complete attendance data are available, they attended class an average of 3.05 out of 6 days, compared to 4.39 days for other students). They received poorer semester grades (averaging a 1.92 on the 4-point scale, compared to 2.86 for the other students). We would not expect students who participate minimally in the simulations and perform poorly in the class to experience the skills gains and attitude changes experienced by those who excelled in the class; these results bear out this expectation.

It remains an open question as to *why* this group of students performed so poorly. Impressionistically, the African American females in the class this academic year seemed a weaker group of students than was typical of African American females I have taught in the past. For comparative purposes, the grade gap between African American women and the rest of the class was nowhere near as large in my classes the two previous years. It is possible that the performance of this group of African American females reflected an unlucky random draw from the distribution of students, perhaps exacerbated by a relatively small number of students on which this analysis is based.

More troubling, however, is the possibility that this effect is not random but rather reflects a systematic problem with my approach. The course design clearly and intentionally removes students from their comfort zone; the political skills being developed here require students to be at least somewhat outgoing and project a certain amount of confidence in their opinions. It may also be that the simulation replicates the dynamics of the larger world, leading African American women to feel silenced in the simulation and powerless to disrupt. For African American students, particularly women, these activities may expose a lack of self-confidence and lead to withdrawal from class activities. Thus it may be that what I ask of students puts the most vulnerable of them at risk, manifested in less engagement with the class and hence poorer performance. These possibilities will be examined in future iterations of the course and in my future explorations of student performance therein.

There is much to recommend the approach I use. Normatively, I believe citizenship education is a better way to take advantage of my one chance to reach these students politically and civically. Empirically, I demonstrate here that most students end up more confident in their political skills and more efficacious as a result of these simulations. Ensuring that *all* students benefit from an approach like this remains the most significant challenge facing me in teaching this course into the future.

NEW DIRECTIONS FOR TEACHING AND LEARNING • DOI: 10.1002/tl

# References

Bennett, S. E. "The Past Need Not Be Prologue: Why Pessimism About Civic Education Is Premature." *PS: Political Science and Politics*, 1999, 32(4), 755–757.

Bernstein, J. L. "Cultivating Civic Competence: Simulations and Skill-Building in an Introductory Government Class." *Journal of Political Science Education,* forthcoming.

Calder, L. "Uncoverage: Toward a Signature Pedagogy for the History Survey." *Journal of American History,* 2006, 92(4), 1358–1370.

Cuban, L. *How Scholars Trumped Teachers: Change Without Reform in University Curriculum, Teaching, and Research, 1890–1990.* New York: Teachers College Press, 1999.

Davis, D. W., and Silver, B. D. "Stereotype Threat and Race of Interviewer Effects in a Survey on Political Knowledge." *American Journal of Political Science,* 2003, 47(1), 33–45.

Delli Carpini, M. X., and Keeter, S. "Stability and Change in the U.S. Public's Knowledge of Politics." *Public Opinion Quarterly,* 1991, 55(4), 583–612.

Delli Carpini, M. X., and Keeter, S. *What Americans Know About Politics and Why It Matters.* New Haven, Conn.: Yale University Press, 1996.

Dewey, J. *The Public and Its Problems.* Athens, Ohio: Swallow Press, 1954. (Originally published 1927.)

Downs, A. *An Economic Theory of Democracy.* New York: HarperCollins, 1957.

Frantzich, S. E. *Citizen Democracy: Political Activists in a Cynical Age* (2nd ed.). Lanham, Md.: Rowman & Littlefield, 2005.

Lupia, A., and McCubbins, M. D. *The Democratic Dilemma: Can Citizens Learn What They Need to Know?* New York: Cambridge University Press, 1998.

Mann, H. "Twelfth Annual Report to the Massachusetts Board of Education." In L.A. Cremin (ed.), *The Republic and the School: Horace Mann on the Education of Free Men.* New York: Teachers College Press, 1957.

Popkin, S. L. *The Reasoning Voter: Communication and Persuasion in Presidential Campaigns.* Chicago: University of Chicago Press, 1991.

Rapoport, R. B. "The Sex Gap in Political Persuading: Where the 'Structuring Principle' Works." *American Journal of Political Science,* 1981, 25(1), 32–48.

Rosenstone, S. J., and Hansen, J. M. *Mobilization, Participation, and Democracy in America.* Old Tappan, N.J.: Macmillan, 1993.

Teixeira, R. A. *The Disappearing American Voter.* Washington, D.C.: Brookings Institution, 1992.

Verba, S., Burns, N., and Schlozman, K. L. "Knowing and Caring About Politics: Gender and Political Engagement." *Journal of Politics,* 1997, 59(4), 1051–1072.

Wiggins, G., and McTighe, J. *Understanding by Design.* Alexandria, Va.: Association for Supervision and Curriculum Development, 1998.

Zaller, J. *The Nature and Origins of Mass Opinion.* New York: Cambridge University Press, 1992.

JEFFREY L. BERNSTEIN *is an associate professor of political science at Eastern Michigan University. He was a 2005–06 Carnegie Scholar in the Carnegie Academy for the Scholarship of Teaching and Learning (CASTL).*

# 12

*How can disciplines that are commonly regarded as culturally neutral be taught in ways that connect technical content with social and cultural issues?*

# Infusing Mathematics with Culture: Teaching Technical Subjects for Social Justice

*Dale Winter*

Quantitative methods and logical reasoning provide tools for making informed judgments about situations encountered in everyday life—the arena of cultural and social phenomena. Despite this, academic encounters with social and cultural issues are rare in the lecture halls and laboratories of STEM (science, technology, engineering, and mathematics) disciplines (Miller, 2005), the disciplines that traditionally emphasize training in quantitative analyses and logical thinking (English and Halford, 1995).

For more than twenty years the undergraduate mathematics teaching community has conducted a deep conversation concerning the pedagogies appropriate for introductory mathematics courses, including college algebra, precalculus, and calculus (Ganter, 2000, 2001). Fueling this ongoing discussion has been the recognition that students' failure to "acquire a deep understanding of the material they are supposed to learn in their [mathematics] courses" (Graesser, Person, and Hu, 2002, p. 33) is still unacceptably common (Bookman and Friedman, 1994; Selden, Mason, and Selden, 1989; Smith, 1998).

This conversation has produced changes in the pedagogy of many mathematics courses (Hurley, Koehn, and Ganter, 1999; Lutzer, Maxwell, and Rodi, 2002), including increased use of cooperative learning and technology to promote learning. Recognizing the value of student interest as a

NEW DIRECTIONS FOR TEACHING AND LEARNING, no. 111, Fall 2007  © Wiley Periodicals, Inc.
Published online in Wiley InterScience (www.interscience.wiley.com) • DOI: 10.1002/tl.291

resource for learning (Schiefele and Csikszentmihalyi, 1995), many instructors have highlighted the applicability and usefulness of mathematical techniques for solving problems in the world outside the classroom (see Alper, Fendel, Fraser, and Resek, 1996; De Bock and others, 2003; Forman and Steen, 2000; Pollack, 1978; Walkerdine, 1988). One rationale for integrating social and cultural learning with traditional STEM learning is to use undergraduates' enthusiasm for social and political issues (National Survey of Student Engagement, 2004) as an engine to drive more abstract and conceptual mathematical learning (Carter and Brickhouse, 1989; Nix, Ryan, Manly, and Deci, 1999; Zoller, 1990).

## A Model for Integrating Social and Cultural Issues into STEM Learning

The fundamental goal of any STEM course must be to involve students in the acquisition and mastery of the knowledge, skills, and perspectives of a technical discipline (Hauser, 2006). My model (see Figure 12.1) intertwines the technical learning characteristic of STEM disciplines with experiences and information to allow students to make better sense of some of the challenges and problems faced by other peoples and other cultures. This approach presents some immediate instructional challenges. For example, the understandable drive to emphasize STEM content in a STEM course might lead to a trivialization of the social and cultural studies aspects of the course (Cooper, 1992; Pollack, 1978). Wiest (2002) notes that incorporating cultural and social content into mathematics instruction might well be considered "inappropriate . . . if the [cultural] content is merely grafted onto a topic . . . or treated superficially" (p. 49). To help to avoid trivialization, I have followed one of the models suggested by Wiest, studying social and cultural issues using precalculus mathematical concepts as a tool.

In practical terms, implementation of this approach involved introducing sociocultural phenomena through collections of readings (including photographs and maps where appropriate), short video clips illustrating key aspects of each situation, and activities or games that the students would engage with as preparation for their mathematical work. When the students had become acquainted with the social situation, a problem or question would be posed to them and a structured worksheet provided to guide students through the intellectual process of developing mathematical tools to make better sense of the social problem (see Figure 12.1).

Students' newly acquired knowledge of social problems and cultural ideas was intertwined with mathematical ideas they could apply to represent salient features of the situation mathematically, reformulate the problem in mathematical terms (see Figure 12.1), and use the mathematical ideas that they had learned to solve the problem.

Upon solving the mathematical version of the problems, students completed a cycle of learning by interpreting the meaning of their mathemati-

**Figure 12.1. Interplay Between Mathematical, Social, and Cultural Learning.**

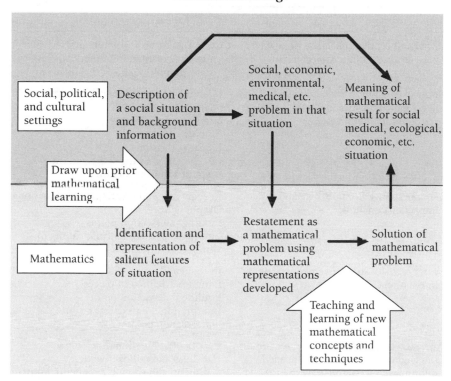

cal solution in the context that they had begun with, often leading to discussion of the broader implications of their solution. This was particularly the case in controversial examples such as deciding on the best course of action for using limited public funds in the fight against HIV/AIDS in Uganda.

To illustrate the learning activities that were used, an example follows. (A complete list of the topics and the mathematical concepts involved is provided in Table 12.1.)

## Native Peoples' Rights and Fresh Water in Botswana

This learning activity used the context of water rights in Botswana as motivation for the mathematical concepts of piecewise defined functions, domain, and range.

Students began this activity with a short, informal general knowledge quiz about countries in sub-Saharan Africa. The answers to many of these

### Table 12.1. Topics Covered Using Enhanced Learning Activities During the Course

| Social Problem | Mathematical Concepts Involved |
|---|---|
| Racial and gender imbalance in new HIV infection rates in the United States | Comprehension and integration of information presented in numerical, algebraic, graphical, and verbal formats |
| Political corruption and economic development in Africa, Southeast Asia, Europe, and South America | Manipulation and analysis of numerical data<br>Graphing data points<br>Finding patterns<br>Linear regression<br>Interpretation of the slope and intercept of a linear function |
| Climate change in Zimbabwe and the impact on agriculture | Recognizing and creating linear functions<br>Graphing linear functions<br>Finding intersection points<br>Interpreting the practical meaning of intersection points |
| Water security and native peoples' rights in Botswana | Domain and range of a function<br>Functions defined in pieces<br>Finding intersection points<br>Interpreting the practical meaning of intersection points |
| Ancestral lands and petroleum resources: the Uighur minority and redheaded mummies of western China | Exponential functions<br>Half-lives and radioactive decay<br>Setting up and solving exponential functions numerically and with logarithms |
| Estimating the impact of chemical fertilizers in sub-Saharan Africa | Quadratic functions in standard and vertex form<br>Quadratic regression<br>Completing the square<br>Locating the vertex of a quadratic function and interpreting its meaning |
| The global disease burden of malaria | Power, exponential, and logarithmic functions<br>Logarithmic transformations of data<br>Estimating the model parameters in power regression<br>Setting up and solving power equations |
| The cost of providing ARV medications in Uganda | Power functions<br>Combining functions to produce new functions<br>Laws of exponents and algebra<br>Setting up and solving power equations<br>Finding intersection points for power graphs |

*(continued)*

## Table 12.1. (continued)

| Social Problem | Mathematical Concepts Involved |
| --- | --- |
| How quickly can polio be eradicated? Medical, political, economic, and social factors | Formulas for polynomial functions<br>Recognizing polynomial functions from graphs<br>Polynomial regression<br>Locating the zeros of a polynomial function |
| Milestones in the HIV/AIDS pandemic | Patterns in data<br>Recognizing linear, exponential, and polynomial functions<br>Regression<br>Graphing and interpreting inverses<br>The horizontal line test<br>Finding formulas for inverses of linear and exponential functions |

quiz questions painted a dim economic picture for the region and highlighted the day-to-day struggles of people who lived on a total income of a few hundred dollars per year, such as obtaining adequate health care. The one exception to this that emerged from the quiz was the nation of Botswana.

The quiz was followed by a short PowerPoint presentation on Botswana highlighting the importance of diamonds for the country's comparatively high per capita gross domestic product (GDP) and the importance of diamond mining for the provision of health care to miners and their families. Also featured, through a series of satellite photographs showing the recession of Botswana's river and lake systems over time, was the fact that Botswana faces a serious shortage of fresh water.

In groups of three or four, students worked on a handout that gave data on the likelihood of Botswana's depleting its water supplies in the next twenty-five years. Students graphed these data and found a linear function to represent them. In a full-class discussion, students considered whether or not a single linear function could accurately represent the data and whether or not a pair of linear functions could do a better job. When students had found a pair of linear functions that worked well, the class was again brought together to consider the question of how to specify the years when each of the two linear functions was appropriate to use, leading to the identification of the mathematical concept of the domain of a function. Students were then asked to use their linear functions to determine the year in which Botswana will definitely run out of fresh water and to decide whether or not the behavior of their linear function accurately represented the situation after that year. Students concluded that once the likelihood reached 100 percent, it should remain at that level rather than continuing to rise (as the linear function did). With this, a third, horizontal part was added to the function defined in pieces that the students had created, and the mathematical concept of range (the set of meaningful values generated by a function) was identified.

When the students had finished these calculations, the PowerPoint presentation resumed with a list of historical events from Botswana. One particular point that was greeted with verbal incredulity by students was the fact that until the middle of the twentieth century, it had been legal to hunt the native San people and that the last official license to do so was issued in 1936. This point generated a significant class discussion on the fairness with which the San people had been treated by European colonial powers and continued to be treated by the government of Botswana. This discussion continued with the observation that to maintain its economy, Botswana is under pressure to find new diamond mines but that the most promising lands are those unsuitable for agriculture or urban development that the San have been forced onto. The activity concluded by examining some of the evidence of current government efforts to force the San from potential diamond mines—ironically, by destroying the San people's fresh water supplies (U.S. Department of State, 2005).

## Key Features of the Learning Activities

Marilyn Frankenstein (1990) pioneered the use of mathematical learning through the study of sociocultural phenomena by undergraduates, developing a series of mathematical learning activities in which students were encouraged to "confront various . . . issues while simultaneously learning basic mathematics" (p. 338). Important principles derived from Frankenstein concerning essential features of the nonmathematical learning activities in this project included the following.

*Real situations and real information.* Students were expected to spend a significant amount of time and effort learning about the nonmathematical context of the situation. Invented or contrived situations seemed to us unlikely to capture students' imaginations or to present them with an authentic nonmathematical learning experience (du Feu, 2001).

*Situations that students might have encountered through news or other media sources but were unlikely to be well informed about.* Students' own knowledge or experience was an important touchstone to help the nonmathematical aspects of learning activities gain credibility. As the goals of this course included stimulating both mathematical and nonmathematical learning, it was also important to provide all students (even those who had some exposure to a particular nonmathematical topic) an opportunity to learn something new.

*Descriptions of contexts that could generate controversy.* An overwhelming priority of many instructors is to eliminate conflicting views or controversies from the classroom (DeCecco and Richards, 1974). However, research in education indicates that properly managed interactions with controversial material can help students increase their curiosity, understand other perspectives more accurately, solve problems more effectively, and generate creative ideas (Johnson and Johnson, 1979). An important goal of this instructional model was to help students engage with the material (mathematics and the nonmathematical context) more deeply, and controversy offered a means to achieve this objective.

## Evaluating the Model for Integrating Social and Cultural Issues into STEM Learning

The instructional model described here was tested with a naturalistic experiment (results will be summarized shortly). Students taught with the culturally infused learning activities were compared to other students in the same course who were taught with more conventional materials. Students in the two groups were compared on mathematical performance, general knowledge, and overall success in the course.

**Experimental Design.** Five separate sections of a precalculus course ($n = 148$) were taught using a mixture of conventional methods and activities including cultural and social contexts. Twenty-three sections in the same course ($n = 593$) were taught using conventional methods. Two-thirds of students (67 percent) completed questionnaires at the beginning and end of the semester. In addition, all students took three uniform mathematics exams (scored using predefined grading rubrics).

**Initial Assessments.** Comparing the ACT math scores of the experimental and control groups revealed no significant differences in initial mathematical ability (the mean for the experimental group was 25.17 and for the control group 25.32). The experimental group included slightly higher percentages of female and minority students, although the differences were not statistically significant.

**Mathematical Performance.** A major concern with this model of STEM instruction is that the large amounts of class time that students spend learning about other cultures could undermine their ability to master the technical content of the course. Two effects have been suggested as important here: the lower amount of mathematical "time on task" experienced by students in the experimental groups (Stallings, 1980; Webb, 1991) and the cognitive "contextual interference effect" (Van Merrienboer, De Croock, and Jelsma, 1997). Students in the control and experimental groups completed exactly the same mathematical exams during the semester (it did not feature any richly contextualized problems), and the exams were all graded in the same way according to predefined rubrics. Repeated measures ANOVA revealed no significant differences in the mean performance of students between the control and experimental groups.

**General Knowledge.** At the beginning and end of the semester, students completed multiple-choice exams on the topics that were included in the culturally infused activities. At the beginning of the semester, the difference in the percentage of questions answered correctly by both groups was an insignificant 0.14 percent. By the end of the semester, the percentage of correct responses from the experimental group exceeded that of the control group by a significant 11.9 percent ($p < .05$).

**Success in the Course.** For the purposes of this experiment, success in the course was defined as course completion with a grade of C minus or higher. The final grades in the precalculus course were determined by the students' scores on the uniform exams and modified up or down by instructors. The percentage of unsuccessful students in the experimental group was 15.4 percent, which was significantly ($p < .05$) lower than the 22.9 percent of unsuccessful students in the control group.

## Impact on Students

Although the statistics indicate that the use of this instructional model increased students' general knowledge without sacrificing mathematical performance, they do not reveal the impact of the activities on individual students. Two anecdotes from the course may indicate some of the ways in which students were affected by the course in less easily quantitatively measured ways.

The first is an unsolicited e-mail received by one of the instructors who taught using these learning activities. The text of the e-mail speaks for itself:

> I wanted to thank you for all your help throughout the semester. I am amazed at how much I was able to learn despite the fact that I took precalculus in high school. Your class was always interesting, and I am still amazed at the things that I learned pertaining to the world at large, and not solely mathematics. I never thought that I would be informed about so many significant and often disturbing issues plaguing our world in a math class. . . . I hope that you already were aware that your students find your teaching techniques refreshingly innovative and helpful. If you weren't, I hope you know now.

The second anecdote concerns the reaction of a group of students from another class that used these learning activities. These students felt so strongly that they wanted to do something concrete and real that they (with the help of their instructors) created a scheme to earn money from sponsors whenever they did well on a math quiz. The money that was collected (over $300 by the end of the semester) was donated to a charity that worked on the kinds of social and health care problems that the students had learned about.

## Summary

This chapter described an instructional model for infusing social and cultural learning into a technical course. It also included evidence to demonstrate that STEM courses can be infused with social and cultural without negatively affecting STEM learning. Learning mathematics with substantial amounts of social and cultural information did not detract from mathematical learning. Furthermore, as noted by Astin (1993), infusing courses with social and cultural content can lead to cognitive learning gains (knowledge of global health care issues). Students in the experimental group were more likely to complete the course and less likely to end the semester with an unacceptable grade than students in the control group. As the experimental group contained a higher number of female students and students from minority groups, one possibility is that the instructional methods and content used here made the mathematics in the class more appealing or more accessible to students who might otherwise have disappeared from or failed the class (Seymour and Hewitt, 2000).

## References

Alper, L., Fendel, D., Fraser, S., and Resek, D. "Problem-Based Mathematics: Not Just for the College-Bound." *Educational Leadership,* 1996, *53*(5), 18–21.

Astin, A. W. *What Matters in College? Four Critical Years Revisited.* San Francisco: Jossey-Bass, 1993.

Bookman, J., and Friedman, C. P. "A Comparison of the Problem-Solving Performance of Students in Lab-Based and Traditional Calculus." In E. Dubinsky, A. H. Schoenfeld, and J. Kaput (eds.), *Research in Collegiate Mathematics Education,* Vol. 1. Providence, R.I.: American Mathematical Society, 1994.

Carter, C. S., and Brickhouse, N. W. "What Makes Chemistry Difficult? Alternate Perceptions." *Journal of Chemical Education,* 1989, *66*(3), 223–225.

Cooper, B. "Testing National Curriculum Mathematics: Some Critical Comments on the Treatment of 'Real' Contexts for Mathematics." *Curriculum Journal,* 1992, *3*(3), 231–243.

De Bock, D., and others. "Do Realistic Contexts and Graphical Representations Always Have a Beneficial Impact on Students' Performance? Negative Evidence from a Study on Modeling Non-Linear Geometry Problems." *Learning and Instruction,* 2003, *13*(4), 441–463.

DeCecco, J., and Richards, A. *Growing Pains: The Uses of School Conflict.* New York: Aberdeen Press, 1974.

du Feu, C. "Naming and Shaming." *Mathematics in School,* 2001, *30*(3), 2–8.

English, L. D., and Halford, G. S. *Mathematics Education: Models and Processes.* Mahwah, N.J.: Erlbaum, 1995.

Forman, S. L., and Steen, L. A. "Beyond Eighth Grade: Functional Mathematics for Life and Work." In M. J. Burke and F. R. Curcio (eds.), *Learning Mathematics for a New Century.* Reston, Va.: National Council of Teachers of Mathematics, 2000.

Frankenstein, M. "Incorporating Race, Gender, and Class Issues into a Critical Mathematics Literacy Curriculum." *Journal of Negro Education,* 1990, *59*(3), 336–347.

Ganter, S. L. (ed.). *Calculus Renewal: Issues for Undergraduate Mathematics Education in the Next Decade.* New York: Kluwer Academic/Plenum, 2000.

Ganter, S. L. *Changing Calculus: A Report on Evaluation Efforts and National Impact from 1988–1998.* MAA Notes no. 56. Washington, D.C.: Mathematical Association of America, 2001.

Graesser, A. C., Person, N. K., and Hu, X. "Improving Comprehension Through Discourse Processing." In D. F. Halpern and M. D. Hakel (eds.), *Applying the Science of Learning to University Teaching and Beyond.* New Directions in Teaching and Learning, no. 89. San Francisco: Jossey Bass, 2002.

Hauser, M. "Parental Guidance Required." In J. Brockman (ed.), *Intelligent Thought.* New York: Vintage Books, 2006.

Hurley, J. F., Koehn, U., and Ganter, S. L. "Effects of Calculus Reform: Local and National." *American Mathematical Monthly,* 1999, *106*(9), 800–811.

Johnson, D. W., and Johnson, R. T. "Conflict in the Classroom: Controversy and Learning." *Review of Educational Research,* 1979, *49*(1), 51–70.

Lutzer, D. J., Maxwell, J. W., and Rodi, S. B. *Statistical Abstract of Undergraduate Programs in the Mathematical Sciences in the United States.* Providence, R.I.: American Mathematical Society, 2002.

Miller, A. T. "The Multicultural Lab: Diversity Issues in STEM Classes." In M. Ouellett (ed.), *Teaching Inclusively.* Stillwater, Okla.: New Forums Press, 2005.

National Survey of Student Engagement. *Student Engagement: Pathways to Collegiate Success.* Bloomington: Indiana University Center for Postsecondary Research, 2004.

Nix, G. A., Ryan, R. M., Manly, J. B., and Deci, E. L. "Revitalization Through Self-Regulation: The Effects of Autonomous and Controlled Motivation on Happiness and Vitality." *Journal of Experimental Social Psychology,* 1999, *35*(2), 266–284.

Pollack, H. O. "On Mathematics Application and Real Problem Solving." *School Science and Mathematics,* 1978, *78*(3), 232–239.

Schiefele, U., and Csikszentmihalyi, M. "Motivation and Ability as Factors in Mathematics Experience and Achievement." *Journal for Research in Mathematics Education,* 1995, *26*(2), 163–181.

Selden, J., Mason, A., and Selden, A. "Can Average Calculus Students Solve Nonroutine Problems?" *Journal of Mathematical Behavior,* 1989, *8*(1), 45–50.

Seymour, E., and Hewitt, N. M. *Talking About Leaving. Why Undergraduates Leave the Sciences.* Boulder, Colo.: Westview Press, 2000.

Smith, D. A. "Renewal in Collegiate Mathematics Education." *Documenta Mathematica,* 1998, *Extra Volume*(3), 777–786.

Stallings, J. "Allocated Academic Learning Time Revisited, or Beyond Time on Task." *Educational Researcher,* 1980, *9*(11), 11–16.

U.S. Department of State. "Botswana: Country Reports on Human Rights Practices, 2004." Feb. 28, 2005. http://www.state.gov/g/drl/rls/hrrpt/2004/41589.htm. Retrieved May 31, 2007.

Van Merrienboer, J.J.G., De Croock, M.B.M., and Jelsma, O. "The Transfer Paradox: Effects of Contextual Interference on Retention and Transfer Performance of a Complex Cognitive Skill." *Perceptual and Motor Skills,* 1997, *84*(1), 784–786.

Walkerdine, V. *The Mastery of Reason.* London: Routledge, 1988.

Webb, N. M. "Task-Related Verbal Interaction and Mathematics Learning in Small Groups." *Journal for Research in Mathematics Education,* 1991, *22*(5), 366–389.

Wiest, L. "Multicultural Mathematics Instruction: Approaches and Resources." *Teaching Children Mathematics,* 2002, *9*(1), 49–50.

Zoller, U. "Students' Misunderstandings and Misconceptions in College Freshmen Chemistry (General and Organic)." *Journal of Research in Science Teaching,* 1990, *27*(9), 1053–1065.

DALE WINTER *is an assistant professor in the Department of Mathematics at the University of Michigan, where he codirects the freshman-sophomore program in mathematics.*

# INDEX

TL107   **Exploring Research-Based Teaching**
*Carolin Kreber*
Investigates the wide scope research-based teaching, while focusing on two
distinct forms. The first sees research-based teaching as student-focused,
inquiry-based learning; students become generators of knowledge. The
second perspective fixes the lens on teachers; the teaching is characterized
by discipline-specific inquiry into the teaching process itself. Both methods
have positive effects on student learning, and this volume explores research
and case studies.
ISBN: 07879-9077-9

TL106   **Supplemental Instruction: New Visions for Empowering Student Learning**
*Marion E. Stone, Glen Jacobs*
Supplemental Instruction (SI) is an academic support model introduced over
thirty years ago to help students be successful in difficult courses. SI teaches
students how to learn via regularly scheduled, out-of-class collaborative
sessions with other students. This volume both introduces the tenets of SI to
beginners and brings those familiar up to speed with today's methods and
the future directions. Includes case studies, how-to's, benefits to students
and faculty, and more.
ISBN: 0-7879-8680-1

TL105   **A Laboratory for Public Scholarship and Democracy**
*Rosa A. Eberly, Jeremy Cohen*
Public scholarship has grown out of the scholarship-and-service model, but
its end is democracy rather than volunteerism. The academy has intellectual
and creative resources that can help build involved, democratic communities
through public scholarship. Chapters present concepts, processes, and case
studies from Penn State's experience with public scholarship.
ISBN: 0-7879-8530-9

TL104   **Spirituality in Higher Education**
*Sherry L. Hoppe, Bruce W. Speck*
With chapters by faculty and administrators, this book investigates the role
of spirituality in educating the whole student while recognizing that how
spirituality is viewed, taught, and experienced is intensely personal. The goal
is not to prescribe a method for integrating spirituality but to offer options
and perspectives. Readers will be reminded that the quest for truth and
meaning, not the destination, is what is vitally important.
ISBN: 0-7879-8363-2

TL103   **Identity, Learning, and the Liberal Arts**
*Ned Scott Laff*
Argues that we must foster conversations between liberal studies and student
development theory, because the skills inherent in liberal learning are the
same skills used for personal development. Students need to experience core
learning that truly influences their critical thinking skills, character
development, and ethics. Educators need to design student learning
encounters that develop these areas. This volume gives examples of how
liberal arts education can be a healthy foundation for life skills.
ISBN: 0-7879-8333-0

TL102   **Advancing Faculty Learning Through Interdisciplinary Collaboration**
*Elizabeth G. Creamer, Lisa R. Lattuca*
Explores why stakeholders in higher education should refocus attention on
collaboration as a form of faculty learning. Chapters give theoretical basis

then practical case studies for collaboration's benefits in outreach, scholarship, and teaching. Also discusses impacts on education policy, faculty hiring and development, and assessment of collaborative work.
ISBN: 0-7879-8070-6

TL101 **Enhancing Learning with Laptops in the Classroom**
*Linda B. Nilson, Barbara E. Weaver*
This volume contains case studies—mostly from Clemson University's leading-edge laptop program—that address victories as well as glitches in teaching with laptop computers in the classroom. Disciplines using laptops include psychology, music, statistics, animal sciences, and humanities. The volume also advises faculty on making a laptop mandate successful at their university, with practical guidance for both pedagogy and student learning.
ISBN: 0-7879-8049-8

TL100 **Alternative Strategies for Evaluating Student Learning**
*Michelle V. Achacoso, Marilla D. Svinicki*
Teaching methods are adapting to the modern era, but innovation in assessment of student learning lags behind. This volume examines theory and practical examples of creative new methods of evaluation, including authentic testing, testing with multimedia, portfolios, group exams, visual synthesis, and performance-based testing. Also investigates improving students' ability to take and learn from tests, before and after.
ISBN: 0-7879-7970-8

TL99 **Addressing Faculty and Student Classroom Improprieties**
*John M. Braxton, Alan E. Bayer*
Covers the results of a large research study on occurrence and perceptions of classroom improprieties by both students and faculty. When classroom norms are violated, all parties in a classroom are affected, and teaching and learning suffer. The authors offer guidelines for both student and faculty classroom behavior and how institutions might implement those suggestions.
ISBN: 0-7879-7794-2

TL98 **Decoding the Disciplines: Helping Students Learn Disciplinary Ways of Thinking**
*David Pace, Joan Middendorf*
The Decoding the Disciplines model is a way to teach students the critical-thinking skills required to understand their specific discipline. Faculty define bottlenecks to learning, dissect the ways experts deal with the problematic issues, and invent ways to model experts' thinking for students. Chapters are written by faculty in diverse fields who successfully used these methods and became involved in the scholarship of teaching and learning.
ISBN: 0-7879-7789-6

TL97 **Building Faculty Learning Communities**
*Milton D. Cox, Laurie Richlin*
A very effective way to address institutional challenges is a faculty learning community. FLCs are useful for preparing future faculty, reinvigorating senior faculty, and implementing new courses, curricula, or campus initiatives. The results of FLCs parallel those of student learning communities, such as retention, deeper learning, respect for others, and greater civic participation. This volume describes FLCs from a practitioner's perspective, with plenty of advice, wisdom, and lessons for starting your own FLC.
ISBN: 0-7879-7568-0

**TL96**     Online Student Ratings of Instruction
*Trav D. Johnson, D. Lynn Sorenson*
Many institutions are adopting Web-based student ratings of instruction, or
are considering doing it, because online systems have the potential to save
time and money among other benefits. But they also present a number of
challenges. The authors of this volume have firsthand experience with
electronic ratings of instruction. They identify the advantages, consider costs
and benefits, explain their solutions, and provide recommendations on how
to facilitate online ratings.
ISBN: 0-7879-7262-2

**TL95**     Problem-Based Learning in the Information Age
*Dave S. Knowlton, David C. Sharp*
Provides information about theories and practices associated with problem-
based learning, a pedagogy that allows students to become more engaged in
their own education by actively interpreting information. Today's professors
are adopting problem-based learning across all disciplines to faciliate a
broader, modern definition of what it means to learn. Authors provide
practical experience about designing useful problems, creating conducive
learning environments, facilitating students' activities, and assessing
students' efforts at problem solving.
ISBN: 0-7879-7172-3

**TL94**     Technology: Taking the Distance out of Learning
*Margit Misangyi Watts*
This volume addresses the possibilities and challenges of computer
technology in higher education. The contributors examine the pressures to
use technology, the reasons not to, the benefits of it, the feeling of being a
learner as well as a teacher, the role of distance education, and the place of
computers in the modern world. Rather than discussing only specific
successes or failures, this issue addresses computers as a new cultural
symbol and begins meaningful conversations about technology in general
and how it affects education in particular.
ISBN: 0-7879-6989-3

**TL93**     Valuing and Supporting Undergraduate Research
*Joyce Kinkead*
The authors gathered in this volume share a deep belief in the value of
undergraduate research. Research helps students develop skills in problem
solving, critical thinking, and communication, and undergraduate
researchers' work can contribute to an institution's quest to further
knowledge and help meet societal challenges. Chapters provide an overview
of undergraduate research, explore programs at different types of
institutions, and offer suggestions on how faculty members can find ways to
work with undergraduate researchers.
ISBN: 0-7879-6907-9

**TL92**     The Importance of Physical Space in Creating Supportive Learning
Environments
*Nancy Van Note Chism, Deborah J. Bickford*
The lack of extensive dialogue on the importance of learning spaces in
higher education environments prompted the essays in this volume. Chapter
authors look at the topic of learning spaces from a variety of perspectives,
elaborating on the relationship between physical space and learning, arguing
for an expanded notion of the concept of learning spaces and furnishings,

talking about the context within which decision making for learning spaces takes place, and discussing promising approaches to the renovation of old learning spaces and the construction of new ones.
ISBN: 0-7879-6344-5

TL91    **Assessment Strategies for the On-Line Class: From Theory to Practice**
*Rebecca S. Anderson, John F. Bauer, Bruce W. Speck*
Addresses the kinds of questions that instructors need to ask themselves as they begin to move at least part of their students' work to an on-line format. Presents an initial overview of the need for evaluating students' on-line work with the same care that instructors give to the work in hard-copy format. Helps guide instructors who are considering using on-line learning in conjunction with their regular classes, as well as those interested in going totally on-line.
ISBN: 0-7879-6343-7

TL90    **Scholarship in the Postmodern Era: New Venues, New Values, New Visions**
*Kenneth J. Zahorski*
A little over a decade ago, Ernest Boyer's *Scholarship Reconsidered* burst upon the academic scene, igniting a robust national conversation that maintains its vitality to this day. This volume aims at advancing that important conversation. Its first section focuses on the new settings and circumstances in which the act of scholarship is being played out; its second identifies and explores the fresh set of values currently informing today's scholarly practices; and its third looks to the future of scholarship, identifying trends, causative factors, and potentialities that promise to shape scholars and their scholarship in the new millennium.
ISBN: 0-7879-6293-7

TL89    **Applying the Science of Learning to University Teaching and Beyond**
*Diane F. Halpern, Milton D. Hakel*
Seeks to build on empirically validated learning activities to enhance what and how much is learned and how well and how long it is remembered. Demonstrates that the movement for a real science of learning—the application of scientific principles to the study of learning—has taken hold both under the controlled conditions of the laboratory and in the messy real-world settings where most of us go about the business of teaching and learning.
ISBN: 0-7879-5791-7

TL88    **Fresh Approaches to the Evaluation of Teaching**
*Christopher Knapper, Patricia Cranton*
Describes a number of alternative approaches, including interpretive and critical evaluation, use of teaching portfolios and teaching awards, performance indicators and learning outcomes, technology-mediated evaluation systems, and the role of teacher accreditation and teaching scholarship in instructional evaluation.
ISBN: 0-7879-5789-5

TL87    **Techniques and Strategies for Interpreting Student Evaluations**
*Karron G. Lewis*
Focuses on all phases of the student rating process—from data-gathering methods to presentation of results. Topics include methods of encouraging meaningful evaluations, mid-semester feedback, uses of quality teams and focus groups, and creating questions that target individual faculty needs and interest.
ISBN: 0-7879-5789-5

# New Directions for Teaching and Learning
## Order Form
### SUBSCRIPTIONS AND SINGLE ISSUES

**DISCOUNTED BACK ISSUES:**

*Use this form to receive **20% off** all back issues of New Directions for Teaching and Learning. All single issues priced at **$23.20** (normally $29.00).*

TITLE      ISSUE NO.    ISBN

_____   _____   _____

_____   _____   _____

_____   _____   _____

***Call 888-378-2537*** *or see mailing instructions below. When calling, mention the promotional code, JB7ND, to receive your discount.*

**SUBSCRIPTIONS:** *(1 year, 4 issues)*

☐ New Order    ☐ Renewal

|  |  |  |
|---|---|---|
| U.S. | ☐ Individual: $80 | ☐ Institutional: $195 |
| Canada/Mexico | ☐ Individual: $80 | ☐ Institutional: $235 |
| All Others | ☐ Individual: $104 | ☐ Institutional: $269 |

***Call 888-378-2537*** *or see mailing and pricing instructions below. Online subscriptions are available at www.interscience.wiley.com.*

Copy or detach page and send to:

**John Wiley & Sons, Journals Dept, 5th Floor**
**989 Market Street, San Francisco, CA 94103-1741**

Order Form can also be faxed to: 888-481-2665

| | |
|---|---|
| Issue/Subscription Amount: $ _____ | **SHIPPING CHARGES:** |
| Shipping Amount: $ _____ | SURFACE    Domestic   Canadian |
| (for single issues only—subscription prices include shipping) | First Item    $5.00    $6.00 |
| **Total Amount:** $ _____ | Each Add'l Item   $3.00    $1.50 |

(No sales tax for U.S. subscriptions. Canadian residents, add GST for subscription orders. Individual rate subscriptions must be paid by personal check or credit card. Individual rate subscriptions may not be resold as library copies.)

☐ Payment enclosed (U.S. check or money order only. All payments must be in U.S. dollars.)

☐ VISA ☐ MC ☐ Amex # _____ Exp. Date _____

Card Holder Name _____ Card Issue # _____

Signature_____ Day Phone _____

☐ Bill Me (U.S. institutional orders only. Purchase order required.)

Purchase order # _____
        Federal Tax ID13559302    GST 89102 8052

Name_____

Address _____

Phone _____ E-mail _____